Celebrating with

Julienne

by SUSAN CAMPOY

with JULIE CAMPOY and COLLEEN DUNN BATES

photographs by EMILY BROOKE SANDOR

To Paula and Steve
Be inspired !
Best to you
Julie

Foreword by JOACHIM SPLICHAL

Library of Congress Control Number: 2009922992
The following is for reference only:
Campoy, Susan
Celebrating with Julienne / Susan Campoy
p. cm.
Includes index.
ISBN 978-0-9753939-8-7
    1. Cookbook. 2. California - food/cooking
    I. Campoy, Susan. II. Title

First Edition, first printing
Printed by Typecraft Wood & Jones, Pasadena, CA

Designed by Joseph Shuldiner
Recipe Editing by Rochelle Palermo
Food Styling by Basil Friedman
Prop Styling by Robin Turk
Assistant Food Styling by Susan Kucera
Assistant Prop Styling by April Smith
Assistant Photography by Danny Ventrella
Proofreading by Karen Levy
Illustrations by Jim Cross

Published by Prospect Park Books
prospectparkbooks.com

Dedication

To my wonderful daughters, Cynthia, Julie, Lesley, and Jennifer, who have given me more love and support than I ever could have imagined.

And to the memory of my parents, Lucille and Franklin, who are the true inspiration of my culinary passion.

The Campoy daughters dedicate this book to the memory of our beloved mother. She inspired us in many ways, but most importantly, as a role model who created a vocation out of her passion for cooking and entertaining.

— Susan Barbara Campoy —
1939-2009

THE DAUGHTERS CAMPOY, CIRCA 1973: (LEFT TO RIGHT) LESLEY, CYNTHIA, JENNIFER, AND JULIE

Acknowledgments

Cooking for others is an intensively collaborative undertaking, and so I ask you to bear with me while I thank the many people without whom Julienne never would have succeeded.

First and foremost, thanks to my daughter Julie Campoy, who has been my partner, coworker, and collaborator since 1989. I am so thankful for her hard work, inspiration, dedication, and exuberant spirit, all of which have contributed so much to our success at Julienne.

I'm also deeply grateful to my three other daughters, Cynthia, Lesley, and Jennifer, for doing endless dishes when I began catering out of our home, for making appetizers, for helping me bake, for loading and unloading the station wagon a thousand times, and, most of all, for their continued support. My daughters are my best friends, and I never could have done any of this without them.

My wonderful, creative son-in-law, Brian Brophy, has been a constant source of joy and entertainment in our family. And to my lovely, talented, and beautiful granddaughters, Maeve and Alena, I love you both so much.

Also important to my life and my work are my four sisters, Mary, Vicki, Michelle, and Emmy Lou. I'm grateful to them and their families, who have all been so supportive. We five sisters were blessed with loving parents, and I remember them with gratitude—not just for their love and encouragement, but also for the lessons they taught me about cooking and eating well.

I must thank the endless friends and customers who believed in me, and who kept coming to me with requests for particular dishes and to encourage our expansions. I can't possibly name them all, but a few early ones must be mentioned. Edwina and Tom Johnson gave me one of my first opportunities to cater, and they really launched me. My neighbors Jane and Ron Olson were also early clients, and the legal and business advice Ron has given me over the years has been invaluable. And, of course, untold gratitude to my investors in the early years: Chris and Art Withrow, Richard Ferry, Jim Galbraith, Bill Zimmerman, Bev Sobraske, Carolyn Miller, and Sally DeVore. Without them I literally would not be in business.

Noted graphic designer Jim Cross is responsible for the lovely line drawings of Julienne, which we use to this day.

Thank you to Nancy Moss for graciously allowing us to use her exquisite Moroccan home for the photo shoot of the Moroccan party.

Many thanks are due to the team that helped me create this book: art director and producer Joseph Shuldiner, photographer Emily Brooke Sandor, writer Colleen Dunn Bates, food stylist Basil Friedman, prop stylist Robin Turk, and recipe editor Rochelle Palermo.

The dedication, talent, and loyalty of my employees have made Julienne what it is today. They are talented, dedicated, and loyal, and they are the backbone of our business. A special mention goes to those with the most longevity. Employees with more than thirteen years of tenure include Beverly Beesley, Cristobal Dominguez, Herbert Dominguez, Marcelino Dominguez, Delia Gomez, Hugo Lopez, Anita Machlis, Jose Orellana, and Alfredo Pena Diaz. Employees with nine to thirteen years of tenure include Saul Aviles, Francisco Castro, Ramon Castro, Carlos Cifuentes, Claudia Flores, Juan Perez, Ada Quiroz, and Alessandra Smith. Finally, I must thank the thousands of customers who have brought all of us at Julienne so much business, friendship, inspiration, and satisfaction. Every dish we make, every cookie we bake, every item we stock, and every recipe we now share … they've all been inspired by you.

SUE AND HER GRANDDAUGHTERS, ALENA (LEFT) AND MAEVE

Foreword *2*

Introduction *4*

BRASSERIE

Breakfast *17*

Lunch *31*

GOURMET MARKET

Soups *51*

Sides/Salads *57*

Entrees *69*

Pastries *81*

CELEBRATIONS

Chocolate Festival *103*

A Family Easter *115*

Hollywood Bowl Picnic *125*

An Evening in Morocco *135*

A Harvest Feast *147*

A Winter Celebration *159*

Contributors *170*

Index *172*

Foreword

I first met Susan in 1982 when I was teaching cooking classes at the world-famous Ma Cuisine Cooking School on Melrose. I had been living in the United States for one year and was eager to share the techniques and recipes I had learned while studying with several top chefs in France. Ma Maison the restaurant, was an exciting place to be with celebrities and the "who's who" of show biz flocking to the bistro to sample the freshest ideas from Wolfgang Puck and a team of young European chefs.

Almost immediately, Susan and I realized that we were alike in many ways. We possess a wild culinary imagination, are guided by a fearless entrepreneurial spirit, and love French cooking. Susan approached my classes with outstanding focus as we explored various techniques and dishes. She still recalls my Cold Spring Pea Soup with Yogurt and Mint every time I see her! I was not the least bit surprised when Susan turned her successful catering business into the famous Julienne. Always bustling, Julienne is a cornerstone in the San Marino community where friends gather for coffee or a delicious meal. It is a treat to have Julienne close to my home; I always enjoy stopping in for a bite to eat.

Over the years, Susan and I have become confidantes, comrades, and neighbors. Susan's love of food, dedication to her community, ambition, energy, and life story are most inspiring.

– **Joachim Splichal**
CHEF & FOUNDER, PATINA RESTAURANT GROUP

Introduction

You might say it started with a Brie en croute.

Shortly after I married and began raising a family, I discovered that I loved to entertain. I began reading cookbooks, experimenting with recipes, and hosting luncheons and dinner parties for family and friends. I was also a baker, constantly turning out cookies, bars, tarts, and, at Christmas, elaborate gingerbread houses. Before long, I began taking cooking classes at Ma Cuisine, the school at Los Angeles' acclaimed Ma Maison restaurant. That inspired travels to Italy and France, where I studied at the Cordon Bleu, La Varenne, and Lenôtre.

Early in my culinary studies, I learned to make that icon of early '80s Gourmandise, Brie en croute, and that dish helped me transform from passionate kitchen hobbyist to, eventually, a restaurateur. My friends started asking me to make them the flaky cheese pastries right about the time that I went through a divorce and found myself with a need to make a living. Necessity had sent me back to teaching, for which I had been trained in college, but my heart lived in the kitchen. And when my friends hired me to make hors d'oeuvres for their cocktail parties, I began to think I could make a living doing what I loved.

It was the early '80s, and excitement about food was in the air. My small suburban town, San Marino, was home to people who traveled and had an appreciation for quality food. The same was true for our neighboring city, Pasadena. I was fortunate to be in the right place at the right time. It was only a matter of time until someone asked me to cater a party—in this case, a "very casual" lunch for ten people. I'd hosted dinner parties many times at my home, but never professionally. Nonetheless, I felt up to the challenge.

The hosts were friends from San Marino, Tom and Edwina Johnson. Tom had recently become publisher of the *Los Angeles Times*. It should not have been a surprise when I found out who was on the guest list for this "very casual" lunch—but when I did find out, the day before the party, my anxiety mounted. The guests included well-known and powerful Angelenos, and the guest of honor was Lady Bird Johnson. Clearly I would have to cook a spectacular luncheon—out of my small home kitchen, with no staff and no professional experience. I prepared the meal at home and then served the luncheon at the Johnsons' home.

The luncheon was a success. Among the five courses were individual Bries en croute. Lady Bird Johnson loved the Brie, and asked if I could make one that could travel back to the LBJ ranch in Texas. I went home and made a half-dozen until I deemed one presentable enough for the former First Lady, and I will always remember the day the Secret Service arrived to pick it up for the flight to Texas.

That's when my relationship with food became serious. I was in business as a caterer. I quit substitute teaching, promoted the creaky O'Keefe & Merritt oven with a broken door to heavy use, enlisted my four daughters (Cynthia, Julie, Lesley, and Jennifer, ages 15 to 7) to help load and unload my station wagon, and set out to feed my friends in San Marino, Pasadena, and Los Angeles as well as I possibly could. Given that I had no capital, no staff, and nothing but a home kitchen, this may not have seemed like the most sensible decision; however, my passion for cooking and the support of my friends made it seem at least feasible.

Now that I'm looking back from the perspective of twenty-five years' experience, I can say that not only was it feasible, but it also grew to be successful. Still, when you learn to run a business by trial and error, nothing ever comes easy. Back in those early days, for instance, word got around about the gingerbread houses I helped people make at Christmastime, and 20th Century Fox called to ask if I could make twenty-five of them. My quote was $25 per house (a ridiculously low price, even by standards back then) and I worked feverishly for a week to build those houses. I finished construction and came downstairs the next morning to begin decorating them, only to find that an unsually cold night had caused some of the roofs to slide off.

I rebuilt those houses, of course, and my client was happy. It doesn't take long in the catering business to figure out that you'd better do whatever it takes to make your client happy or you won't be in business for long. And as part of that, you'd better make sure you're working with the best possible people, and treating them with care and respect, because if you can't count on your team when you're throwing a party, you'll be in trouble. You realize that your staff is your biggest asset. In catering, you are only as good as your last party.

After that first "casual" luncheon, I became more adept at catering events. Gradually I expanded my culinary repertoire and learned how to cook for and produce parties for up to 1,000 people. I was fortunate to meet many fascinating, creative, successful people. During this era, for instance, I was asked to be the in-house chef

Lessons Learned

I never really considered myself a "professional" or a "chef," but a mother who loved to cook. I was fortunate enough to take advantage of opportunities that came my way, and that allowed me to pursue my love for entertaining and cooking. Consequently, I had to learn a lot of lessons the hard way. Here are the most essential ones.

☙ **SURROUND YOURSELF WITH THE BEST.** I earned a B.A. in education, and Julie has a degree in journalism. Neither of us trained for this business, so we hired the best people we could afford to handle the tasks we didn't know how to handle.

☙ **HONOR YOUR PASSION.** I was in love with cooking long before I became a professional, and that passion kept me focused and has helped me maintain my commitment to the business. It also helps to have a sense of humor.

☙ **FOLLOW YOUR INTUITION.** Sometimes people said what I wanted couldn't (or shouldn't) be done, but I have not been failed by following my intuition. I paired my intuition, however, with research. The intuitions worth following are the ones that are economically feasible and with which you feel comfortable.

☙ **START SMALL.** Whether starting a restaurant or any other enterprise, start small and expand only when the need dictates. Many people start by opening a very large restaurant, for instance, and they can't sustain the business.

☙ **PUT HONESTY AND INTEGRITY ABOVE ALL.** If you don't maintain your honesty and integrity as a business and a person, neither will amount to much.

☙ **RESPECT YOUR EMPLOYEES.** Not only is it good business practice to build a stable and loyal employee base, but it has also given me great pleasure to see my employees become part of the Julienne family, while growing their own families and successful lives. It has always been important for me to promote from within.

☙ **ACKNOWLEDGE YOUR MISTAKES.** They will happen, and consider them learning experiences. If you admit a mistake and make it up to your customers, they'll be both forgiving and loyal.

☙ **SEEK STRENGTH IN CRISIS.** We all face challenges and crises, and I've certainly had my share. I've learned to see a crisis as a chance to renew myself and grow in ways I never imagined possible.

for Prince Phillip and Princess Anne when they came to L.A. for the 1984 Olympics, as part of the British equestrian team, which was a great thrill.

Eventually, after five years of professional cooking, I found myself with a substantial business and a vastly inadequate home kitchen. So in 1985, I moved into a 1,000-square-foot space on tree-lined Mission Street in San Marino. During a trip to Paris with my friends Art and Chris Withrow, who became my original business partners, I fell in love with the brasserie Julien. To name our catering business and four-table restaurant, we started with "Julien" as inspiration and settled on "Julienne," an homage to both the renowned French brasserie and the essential culinary technique of julienning ingredients.

Not long after we opened Julienne, the Withrows left, and a team of friends—Richard Ferry, Jim Galbraith, Bill Zimmerman, Bev Sobraske, Carolyn Miller, and Sally DeVore—came in as investors. To these people I will be forever grateful. I had little business experience and had never even taken an accounting class, so they were tremendously helpful. With their help, in 1987 I expanded into a neighboring space. In 1989, my daughter Julie joined forces with me, building up our line of takeout foods, just ahead of the era when busy young professionals sought out quality takeout. The gourmet market continued to expand, and before long we were desperate for more room. In 1992, an adjacent space became available, and Julie and I decided to lease it to expand the market. To fund the expansion, I had to borrow against my house—which many thought was risky, given that the country was in the midst of a recession. But I knew it was the right thing to do, so I took out the loan, bought out my wonderful investors, and expanded. In 1997, we expanded once more, adding a private dining room and enlarging the kitchen.

During that time came a new and formidable challenge: breast cancer. I was diagnosed in late 1995 and spent that Christmas starting chemotherapy. Over the next few years, I worked hard to stay healthy while running a bustling catering business, breakfast-and-lunch bistro, and gourmet marketplace, not to mention spending untold hours in city meetings and hearings for each expansion, as well as coping with contractors and construction problems. Something had to give, and it was not going to be my life.

Because the market was increasingly successful, we stopped doing off-site catering in 2000. Julie continued to grow and refine the market, and I focused on what has always mattered most to me: creating the recipes. Working with my wonderful, loyal, longtime staff to develop and finesse our cuisine and make sure our customers eat very well is as much a joy as it ever was. For as was the case when I was making those first Bries en croute back in 1980, the customers are my friends, my neighbors, my family … and there is no better expression of caring for one's friends and family than serving them a comforting meal.

I believe that the focus on our customers has had as much to do with our success as our food. We know so many of them by name. We know who's celebrating a birth or mourning a death. We even see some of our customers two or three times a day. For this reason Julie and I have said no to the many offers to expand to new locations. It's about the quality of our food and the quality of our lives, and we feel that both would suffer if we left our home turf to try to build an empire.

My goal with this book is to inspire. For some, the inspiration might be to bake brownies for your children; for others, it might be to throw that dinner party you've always wanted to throw. A hardy few of you might even be inspired to open that restaurant, start that bakery, or set up shop as a caterer. However you use this book, I encourage you to follow your passion and trust your instincts. For through all my ups and downs, it was following my passion and trusting my instincts that made my cooking—and my business—resonate with my friends, family, and neighbors.

Brasserie

BREAKFAST

Maple Bran Muffins *17*

Crème Brûlée French Toast with Crème
Anglaise and Fresh Berry Coulis *19*

Open-Face Omelet with Roasted
Rosemary Potatoes and
Chicken Sausage *21*

Blueberry Pancakes with Lemon Curd *22*

Candied Applewood Bacon *23*

Callebaut Hot Chocolate *25*

Spinach Crusted Quiche
with Roasted Vegetables *26*

Raspberry Cream Cheese Muffins *27*

Espresso Coffee Cake *29*

LUNCH

Croque Monsieur
with Tomato-Apricot Chutney *31*

Warm Filet of Beef Sandwich with
Caramelized Onions, Gorgonzola Cream
and Arugula on Seeded Sourdough *33*

Bourride with Grilled Vegetables
and Saffron Aïoli *35*

Chopped Salad with Roast-Chicken and
Vegetables and Basil-Parsley Pesto *37*

Grilled Shrimp, Asparagus, and Butter
Lettuce Salad with Mango-Papaya Salsa
and Vanilla Bean Vinaigrette *39*

Parmesan-Crusted Swordfish with
Lemon and Crispy Caper Sauce *40*

The journey to become a restaurateur began in my childhood home in Arcadia, where food mattered. Our house sat on a two-acre lot filled with fruit trees, from which my mother made wonderful preserves. She was also a fine cook, turning out the robust American home cooking of that era. My father made his living in a kitchen, first as a cook for others, then as the owner of Frank's Place, a breakfast-and-lunch café in downtown Los Angeles. They both took care and pride in their cooking, and they had strong opinions about how dishes should be made and presented—but they didn't always agree. In their later years, for instance, our Thanksgiving dinner featured two turkeys. They could never agree on the best way to cook a turkey, so they each made one as part of our annual harvest feast.

By the time I was raising my own family, I was an avid amateur chef, studying the cuisines of the world at the best cooking schools I could find and afford. One of these teachers was Michael Roberts, chef at Trumps (one of Los Angeles' most important restaurants of the era), and he invited me to work in his kitchen for a few days. I was ecstatic. Emboldened by that experience, I impulsively and unsuccessfully tried to get a job in one of L.A.'s most elegant French restaurants and was told to "get out of the kitchen," because I was a woman and an American. I look back on that experience now and cannot believe how naïve and presumptuous I was. But it all came out of a love for cooking.

At that time, the first women were breaking the sexism barrier in restaurant kitchens, but I was not up for the formidable challenge. As friends started asking me to cook for them, I gradually found myself becoming a caterer. Eventually I built up my customer base, found partners with capital, and, in 1985, opened my own restaurant. True, it was little more than a deli counter, a kitchen, and four tables, and at first we served only lunch, but nonetheless, I was a real restaurant chef.

Julienne began life as a French bistro (named for the great Parisian brasserie Julien, which I'd admired on a trip to Paris), but I soon realized that traditional bistro fare was a little too heavy for my California clientele. I reached back to the comfort food of my youth, adding a few modern touches and making sure to have the best possible ingredients, and the result connected with diners. Before long we added breakfast, and for more than twenty years we've been serving breakfast and lunch six days a week—sometimes to guests who dine with us daily.

Julienne's early era, in the mid- to late 1980s, was a time of great creativity and excitement for me: going to the produce, meat, and fish markets; getting to know the purveyors, farmers, and local producers; and, above all, spending lots of time in the kitchen. Julienne became known for twists on classics. The Croque Monsieur, for instance, came about by experimenting in the kitchen. I took the classic French ham-and-cheese sandwich as a starting point, then added Julienne's already-popular tomato-apricot chutney … and, for good measure, I added the basil-parsley pesto. It sure didn't sound like it would work, but it did, and it remains one of our most popular dishes.

Managing a restaurant entails more than just dreaming up flavorful dishes. Customer service is the cornerstone of the business. This is also true for catering, so when I started Julienne I already knew the importance of making customers happy. That's why Julie and I are always on-site, that's why I taste everything, and that's why I designed my office to look into the kitchen. Home cooks can make a dish differently every time, but we have to be consistent day in and day out, so our customers get what they expect.

Over time, as the restaurant, takeout, and catering businesses grew, I had to move off the kitchen line to run the business; I was fortunate to find, nurture, and promote an excellent staff to prepare the meals. But I never left the kitchen completely—to this day my happiest moments are spent at the stove, seeing what happens when you try something new. In the pages that follow you'll discover my very favorite breakfast, lunch, and dessert dishes, some of which are faithful renditions of my mother's classics and others of which resulted from never-ending experimentation. I love them all.

MAPLE BRAN MUFFINS

We like to think this longtime favorite is a bit more healthful than your average muffin. It definitely appeals to our health-conscious customers, thanks to its generous helping of bran. But despite the bran, it's a remarkably light, airy, and moist breakfast treat.

~ MAKES 10 MUFFINS ~

1	cup cake flour
¾	teaspoon baking soda
1½	cups pure maple syrup
1	cup sour cream
¾	cup sugar
4	extra-large eggs
3	cups wheat bran
¾	cup (1½ sticks) unsalted butter, melted

Preheat the oven to 350°F. Line 10 jumbo muffin cups with paper liners. Sift the flour and baking soda into a medium bowl. Whisk the maple syrup, sour cream, sugar, and eggs in another large bowl to blend. Stir in the flour mixture. Mix in the wheat bran, then the melted butter.

Divide the batter evenly among the prepared muffin cups. Bake until a tester inserted into the center of a muffin comes out with some crumbs attached and the tops are brown and crackle slightly, about 35 minutes. Transfer the pan to a rack and set aside until the muffins cool slightly. Remove the muffins from the pan and serve warm, or transfer the muffins to the rack to cool completely.

DO AHEAD: These muffins are best eaten the day they are made. If storing them for 1 to 2 days, cool them completely, then enclose them in an airtight container and keep at room temperature.

CRÈME BRÛLÉE FRENCH TOAST
with CRÈME ANGLAISE and FRESH BERRY COULIS

The huge popularity of this dish always surprises me, because it is so incredibly rich and decadent. We tried to take it off the menu once, and there was a revolt! Sometimes our guests order it as a breakfast "dessert" and share it among the table. We serve it with a raspberry coulis, but you can use pure maple syrup or your favorite jam, or, for a fall variation, sauté some apples with butter, sugar, and cinnamon. Be sure to use an extra-deep baking dish for this recipe—it's really more of a bread pudding than a traditional French toast.

~ SERVES 8 TO 12 ~

CARAMEL:

- 1 cup (packed) dark brown sugar
- 1 cup (2 sticks) unsalted butter
- 1 tablespoon light corn syrup

FRENCH TOAST:

- 15 extra-large eggs
- 3 cups heavy cream
- 1½ cups half-and-half
- ¼ cup Grand Marnier or other orange liqueur
- 1 tablespoon vanilla extract
- 1 vanilla bean, split lengthwise
- 1 1¼-pound loaf French bread, cut into ¾-inch-thick slices
- Crème Anglaise (see following recipe)
- Fresh Berry Coulis (see following recipe)
- Fresh raspberries, for garnish

TO MAKE THE CARAMEL: Whisk the brown sugar, butter, and corn syrup in a heavy medium saucepan over medium heat until the ingredients are melted and well blended. Simmer until the sauce thickens and darkens slightly, whisking occasionally, about 15 minutes. Pour the caramel into a 13 x 9 x 3-inch baking dish and set aside to cool completely.

TO MAKE THE FRENCH TOAST: Whisk the eggs, cream, half-and-half, Grand Marnier, and vanilla extract in a large bowl to blend. Scrape the seeds from the vanilla bean into the custard. Reserve the bean for another use.

Arrange enough of the bread slices on top of the caramel to form a single layer, trimming the bread to fit if necessary. Pour half of the custard over the bread and gently press the bread to submerge it in the custard. Arrange a second layer of bread slices on top of the first layer, then pour the remaining custard over, pressing again to submerge the bread in the custard. Set aside for 1 hour to allow the bread to absorb the custard.

DO-AHEAD: The French toast can be made up to this point 1 day ahead. Cover and refrigerate.

Preheat the oven to 350°F. Bake the bread pudding uncovered until it puffs in the center and becomes golden brown on top, about 45 minutes. Cut the bread pudding into squares and invert the squares onto plates so that the caramel side is on top. Spoon the remaining caramel sauce from the baking dish over each serving. Pour the crème anglaise over each serving. Broil until the crème anglaise begins to brown in spots, about 1 minute. Drizzle the berry coulis alongside each serving. Garnish with raspberries and serve.

continued on next page

CRÈME ANGLAISE

You'll find a million uses for this classic dessert sauce beyond this French toast: drizzle it over fresh berries, pair it with a chocolate flourless cake, or even pour it into an ice cream maker and churn it to make homemade vanilla ice cream.

MAKES ABOUT 4½ CUPS

½   cup sugar

10   extra-large egg yolks

2   vanilla beans, split lengthwise

2   cups heavy cream

2   cups whole milk

Combine the sugar and yolks in a large bowl. Scrape the seeds from the vanilla beans into the sugar mixture. Reserve the beans for another use. Whisk the sugar mixture to blend well.

    Heat the cream and milk in a heavy medium saucepan over medium heat until small bubbles appear around the edges of the pan. Remove the pan from the stove and whisk half of the milk mixture into the egg mixture in a slow steady stream. Slowly whisk the yolk mixture into the remaining milk mixture in the saucepan. Whisk constantly over medium-low heat until the custard thickens enough to coat a spoon, about 5 minutes. Strain the custard through a fine sieve and into a large bowl. Cover and refrigerate.

DO AHEAD: The crème anglaise can be made 2 days ahead. Keep refrigerated.

FRESH BERRY COULIS

A coulis is simply a fruit puree that's used as a sauce. This berry coulis can be made with whatever fruit you have: raspberries, blueberries, strawberries, or blackberries. We use raspberries with the Crème Brûlée French Toast (page 19), and we like a combination of raspberries and blackberries to drizzle over the Blackberry Polenta Bread Pudding (page 81).

MAKES ABOUT 1 CUP

3   cups (about 8 ounces) fresh raspberries, blueberries, strawberries, or blackberries

3   tablespoons (about) sugar

Blend the berries and 3 tablespoons of sugar in a food processor just until pureed. Strain the puree through a fine-meshed strainer and into a small saucepan. Cook over medium heat, stirring, until the sugar dissolves and the sauce simmers. Serve warm, at room temperature, or cold.

DO AHEAD: Cover and refrigerate up to 3 days. If serving the coulis warm, stir it over medium heat to rewarm.

This is a hearty one-skillet dish that comes together within a matter of minutes. This one uses Roasted Rosemary Potatoes (see below) and cooked sausage, but you can get creative and add other meats, such as cooked bacon or diced ham, as well as any leftover roasted vegetables from the night before.

~ SERVES 2 ~

4	teaspoons olive oil, divided
8	ounces chicken Italian sausages, casings removed
2	teaspoons butter
6	extra-large eggs, beaten to blend
	Roasted Rosemary Potatoes, warm (see following recipe)
6	ounces shredded Gruyère cheese
¼	cup finely diced seeded tomato
1	tablespoon chopped fresh chives

Heat 2 teaspoons of oil in a heavy medium skillet over medium-high heat. Add the sausage and cook until golden brown and cooked through, breaking the sausage into large pieces with a wooden spoon, about 4 minutes. Set aside.

DO AHEAD: The sausage can be prepared 1 day ahead. Store in an airtight container and refrigerate. Rewarm before using it in the omelets.

Preheat the broiler. Heat 1 teaspoon of butter and 1 teaspoon of oil in each of two 8-inch nonstick sauté pans over medium heat. Add the beaten eggs to the skillets, dividing equally. Cook until the eggs are set on the bottom but just slightly undercooked on top, lifting the cooked portion of the eggs from the bottom of the skillets to allow the uncooked eggs to run under the cooked portion, about 1½ minutes. Remove the skillets from the heat. Scatter the potatoes and sausage over the eggs, dividing them equally between both skillets. Sprinkle the cheese over the omelets.

Broil just until the cheese melts, about 1 minute. Slide each omelet onto a plate. Sprinkle the tomato and chives over the omelets and serve.

ROASTED ROSEMARY POTATOES

These potatoes are a popular side dish on our breakfast menu, but when teamed with the sausage, they go into this fabulous omelet, too. You can double or triple the recipe to serve more people.

SERVES 2

6	small (1½-inch-diameter) red-skinned potatoes, quartered
1	tablespoon olive oil
1½	teaspoons coarsely chopped fresh rosemary
	Salt and freshly ground black pepper

Preheat the oven to 400°F. Toss the potatoes, oil, and rosemary in a medium bowl to coat. Place the potatoes on a heavy baking sheet and sprinkle with salt and pepper. Roast until the potatoes are tender and golden brown, tossing occasionally to ensure they brown evenly, about 35 minutes.

BLUEBERRY PANCAKES *with* LEMON CURD

We created these pancakes to show off our own lemon curd, which is the real star of this breakfast show. You can sandwich generous dollops of the lemon curd between the pancakes or simply spoon it on top, followed by fresh blueberries (thawed frozen ones work well, too). Making batter from scratch is not difficult to do, especially if you mix the dry ingredients the night before, then add the liquid ingredients in the morning. Pancake purists can substitute pure maple syrup and butter for the lemon curd.

~ SERVES 4 ~

2   cups unbleached all-purpose flour
2   tablespoons (packed) dark brown sugar
2   teaspoons baking powder
½   teaspoon baking soda
½   teaspoon salt
2   cups buttermilk
2   extra-large eggs
2   tablespoons canola oil
2   tablespoons (about) unsalted butter
2   cups fresh blueberries
2   cups Lemon Curd (see following recipe)

Whisk the flour, brown sugar, baking powder, baking soda, and salt in a large bowl to blend. Whisk the buttermilk, eggs, and oil in a medium bowl to blend. Stir the wet ingredients into the dry ingredients until a few lumps still remain (don't overmix this batter).

Heat a heavy flat griddle pan over medium heat until hot. Lightly coat the griddle with butter. Working in batches and forming 12 pancakes total, pour about ⅓ cup of the batter for each pancake onto the griddle and top with a few blueberries. Cook until bubbles form on the surface of the pancakes, about 2 minutes. Turn the pancakes over and cook 2 minutes longer. Transfer the pancakes to plates then top with the lemon curd and the remaining blueberries, and serve immediately.

LEMON CURD

Oh, lemon curd! Who doesn't love this thick, tangy, buttery, sweet condiment? It enhances just about anything: scones, fresh berries, trifle, cakes, even pancakes. This is another Julienne staple since day one, and we still make it in small batches. When making curd, the key to a silky smooth con-sistency is stirring the curd constantly and gently to prevent it from curdling.

MAKES 4 CUPS

1   cup fresh lemon juice (from about 5 lemons)
1   cup sugar
6   extra-large eggs
2   tablespoons finely grated lemon
    peel (from about 3 lemons)
1   cup (2 sticks) unsalted butter, cut into pieces

Whisk the lemon juice, sugar, eggs, and lemon peel in a large stainless steel bowl to blend. Add the butter and set the bowl over a saucepan of simmering water. Stir constantly until the curd thickens just enough to coat the back of a spoon lightly, about 5 minutes. Remove the bowl from atop the saucepan and set it in a large bowl of ice water, whisking the curd until cooled and thickened. Strain the curd into a container. Cover and refrigerate for up to 2 weeks.

CANDIED APPLEWOOD BACON

Like freshly baked bread, candied bacon straight from the oven puts an immediate smile on anyone's face. As the bacon cooks, the sugar coating melts and caramelizes, lending a wonderfully sweet, smoky, and salty flavor. It's impossible to eat just one piece. We use a very thick, high-quality applewood-smoked bacon. Look for one without nitrates or nitrites, made from pork that was raised humanely without antibiotics or growth hormones.

~ SERVES 6 ~

¼ cup (packed) dark brown sugar
12 ¼-inch-thick slices applewood-smoked bacon

Preheat the oven to 350°F. Line a rimmed heavy large baking sheet with foil. Pat the brown sugar on top of the bacon slices, using about 1 teaspoon of sugar for each bacon slice. Lay the bacon, sugar side up, on a rack and set the rack on the prepared baking sheet. This will allow the fat from the bacon to drain while the bacon cooks. Bake until the bacon is crisp and golden and the sugar caramelizes, about 25 minutes. Set aside until the bacon becomes crisp.

DO AHEAD: The bacon can be made 2 hours ahead. Keep at room temperature. Broil before serving to rewarm and re-crisp.

CALLEBAUT HOT CHOCOLATE

I fell in love with Ina Garten's hot chocolate, but I couldn't resist the urge to tinker. By adding cream, more bittersweet chocolate, a dash of pure vanilla extract, and a bit less sugar, I altered it slightly to suit my palate, and our customers love it. Be sure to use both milk and bittersweet chocolates—using just one won't give you the richness and fullness that good cocoa should have. But feel free to alter the other ingredients—for instance, you can omit the espresso and cinnamon in favor of orange peel or your favorite liqueur. Topped with whipped cream and a light dusting of cinnamon is how I prefer it, but it's also wonderful all on its own. We use Callebaut chocolate from Belgium, but other high-quality chocolates, such as Lindt, work well, too.

~ **MAKES FOUR 12-OUNCE SERVINGS** ~

4	cups whole milk
1¼	cups heavy cream, divided
6	ounces bittersweet chocolate (56% to 60% cacao), chopped (about ¾ cup)
2	ounces milk chocolate, chopped (about ⅓ cup)
2	tablespoons instant espresso powder
1	tablespoon sugar
1	tablespoon vanilla extract
½	teaspoon ground cinnamon, plus more for garnish

Whisk the milk and ½ cup of the heavy cream in a heavy medium saucepan over medium-high heat until hot. Remove the pan from the heat and add the bittersweet chocolate, milk chocolate, espresso powder, sugar, vanilla, and ½ teaspoon of the cinnamon. Whisk until the chocolates melt and the mixture is well blended. Cover and keep hot.

DO AHEAD: The hot cocoa can be made 2 days ahead. Cover and refrigerate. Rewarm before serving.

Using an electric mixer, beat the remaining ¾ cup of heavy cream in a large bowl until thick and fluffy. Ladle the hot chocolate into four 12-ounce cups. Top with the whipped cream, sprinkle with cinnamon, and serve.

SPINACH CRUSTED QUICHE *with* ROASTED VEGETABLES

We have served this quiche in both our restaurant and our gourmet market every single day since 1985. Sautéed spinach replaces the traditional pastry crust, making it healthier and easier to prepare. Its versatility lies in its ability to be served for breakfast, lunch, or dinner, and at room temperature or warmed. This enduring recipe is a lifesaver, because you can put almost anything in it: tomatoes and basil, sausage and asparagus, salmon and dill…whatever you like and have on hand.

~ SERVES 8 ~

2	teaspoons olive oil
1	pound fresh spinach
4	tablespoons (½ stick) unsalted butter, divided
1½	cups chopped onion
2	zucchini (about 8 ounces total), cut into 1-inch cubes
1	yellow squash (about 5 ounces), cut into 1-inch cubes
1	red bell pepper, cut into 1-inch pieces
1	yellow bell pepper, cut into 1-inch pieces
6	asparagus spears, tough ends trimmed, cut diagonally into 1-inch pieces
2	tablespoons chopped fresh thyme
1½	cups heavy cream
6	extra-large eggs
1	teaspoon salt
1	teaspoon freshly ground black pepper
2	cups grated Gruyère cheese
½	cup grated Parmesan cheese

Preheat the oven to 350°F. Coat a 9-inch-diameter cake pan with some oil. Heat the oil in a heavy large skillet over medium-high heat. Add the spinach and sauté just until wilted, about 3 minutes. Transfer the spinach to a sieve and set it over a bowl to drain. Once the spinach is cool enough to handle, squeeze as much liquid from the spinach as possible. Arrange the spinach over the bottom and up the sides of the prepared pan, patting to form an even layer.

Melt 2 tablespoons of the butter in the same skillet over medium-high heat. Add the onions and sauté until tender and translucent, about 5 minutes. Transfer the onions to a bowl. Melt the remaining 2 tablespoons of butter in the same skillet over medium-high heat. Add the zucchini, squash, bell peppers, asparagus, and thyme. Increase the heat to high and sauté until the vegetables are tender and beginning to brown, about 12 minutes. Mix in the onions. Scatter the vegetables over the spinach. Cool slightly.

Whisk the cream, eggs, salt, and pepper in a large bowl to blend. Stir in the Gruyère cheese. Pour the cream mixture over the vegetables in the cake pan. Sprinkle the Parmesan cheese over the filling.

DO AHEAD: This quiche can be assembled 1 day ahead. Cover and refrigerate.

Set the cake pan on a baking sheet and bake until the filling is softly set in the center and puffed and the top is golden brown, about 45 minutes. Transfer the cake pan on the baking sheet to a rack and cool the quiche for 15 minutes. Pour off any excess liquid. Invert the quiche onto the baking sheet, then invert it onto a platter so the spinach is on the bottom. Cut the quiche into wedges and serve.

RASPBERRY CREAM CHEESE MUFFINS

This rich, spiced muffin boasts both raspberry preserves and a cheesecake-like filling. Everyone loves them.

~ MAKES 12 MUFFINS ~

8	ounces cream cheese, at room temperature
3	tablespoons plus 1½ cups sugar
3	extra-large eggs, divided
1	teaspoon vanilla extract
3	cups unbleached all-purpose flour
4½	teaspoons ground cinnamon
1	tablespoon baking powder
½	teaspoon baking soda
½	teaspoon salt
1¼	cups whole milk
1	cup (2 sticks) unsalted butter, melted
24	fresh raspberries
12	tablespoons raspberry preserves

Preheat the oven to 350°F. Line 12 jumbo muffin cups with paper liners. Using an electric mixer, beat the cream cheese in a large bowl until well blended and smooth. Add 3 tablespoons of the sugar and beat until well blended. Beat in 1 of the eggs and the vanilla. Set the cream cheese mixture aside.

Whisk the remaining 1½ cups of sugar, the flour, cinnamon, baking powder, baking soda, and salt in a large bowl to blend. Whisk the remaining 2 eggs in a small bowl to blend, then stir them into the dry ingredients. Stir in the milk and melted butter.

Place 2 raspberries in each prepared muffin cup. Spoon the batter over the berries in the muffin cups, dividing equally. Spoon 2 tablespoons of the cream cheese mixture on half of each muffin, and spoon 1 tablespoon of the raspberry preserves on the other half of each muffin.

Bake for about 30 minutes, or until the muffins are pale golden on top and a tester inserted into the cake portion comes out with some crumbs attached. As the muffins bake, a portion of the raspberry preserves and cream cheese mixture will sink into the muffins. Transfer the pans to a rack and cool slightly. Remove the muffins from the pan and cool them completely on the rack or serve warm.

DO AHEAD: These muffins are best eaten the day they are made. If storing them 1 to 2 days, cool them completely, then enclose them in an airtight container and keep at room temperature.

Everyone loves the thick espresso glaze on this rich sour cream Bundt cake, which also boasts a generous swirl of espresso inside. The secret to making this cake tender and moist is the cake flour—don't be tempted to substitute any other type of flour.

~ SERVES 12 TO 15 ~

CAKE:

	Nonstick cooking spray
1½	tablespoons water
3	tablespoons instant espresso powder
5	cups cake flour
1	tablespoon baking powder
1½	teaspoons baking soda
1	teaspoon salt
2¼	cups sugar
1	cup (2 sticks) unsalted butter, at room temperature
4	extra-large eggs
1	tablespoon vanilla extract
2¼	cups sour cream

ESPRESSO GLAZE:

3	cups powdered sugar
⅓	cup freshly brewed strong coffee
¼	cup instant espresso powder

TO PREPARE THE CAKE: Preheat the oven to 350°F. Generously spray a 12-cup nonstick Bundt pan with nonstick spray. Mix the espresso powder and water in a medium bowl to blend, then set aside. Sift the flour, baking powder, baking soda, and salt in a large bowl. Using an electric mixer, beat the sugar and butter in another large bowl until fluffy. Add the eggs 1 at a time, beating well after each addition. Mix in the vanilla. Add the flour mixture in 3 additions, alternating with the sour cream in 2 additions. Stir a fourth of the batter (about 2½ cups) into the reserved espresso mixture. Spoon half of the remaining batter into the prepared Bundt pan and spread evenly. Then pour the espresso batter over, allowing it to spread to the edges of the pan. Top with the remaining batter.

Bake until a tester inserted near the center of the cake comes out with some crumbs attached, about 50 minutes. Transfer the cake in the pan to a rack and cool completely. Invert the cake onto the rack.

TO GLAZE THE CAKE: Whisk the powdered sugar, coffee, and espresso powder in a large bowl until well blended and smooth. Transfer the cake to a platter and pour the glaze over the cake.

DO AHEAD: The cake can be made up to 1 day ahead. Cover the cake with a cake dome and store at room temperature.

CROQUE MONSIEUR *with* TOMATO-APRICOT CHUTNEY

Over the years I've had to spend more and more time on administrative duties, but I still find time to play and create in the kitchen—it's one of my greatest joys. This sandwich came out of one of those play sessions. I started with a traditional French croque monsieur and experimented with some of our housemade pestos and chutneys. Eventually I came up with this version, which we serve in the restaurant with hand-cut pommes frites.

~ MAKES 4 ~

- 1¼ cups Basil-Parsley Pesto (see following recipe)
- 8 ½-inch-thick slices sourdough or whole wheat bread
- 10 ounces thinly sliced Jarlsberg, Gruyère, or other Swiss cheese
- 1 pound thinly sliced Black Forest ham
- 1 cup Tomato-Apricot Chutney, warm (see following recipe)
- 6 tablespoons (¾ stick) butter, at room temperature

Spread the pesto over 1 side of each bread slice. Lay half of the cheese over 4 of the bread slices. Top with the ham then the remaining cheese. Spread the chutney over the pesto on the remaining 4 bread slices. Place the bread slices on the sandwiches, chutney side facing down.

Spread the butter over both sides of the sandwiches. Heat a heavy flat griddle pan over medium-low heat. Add the sandwiches and cook until they are golden brown and the cheese has melted, about 4 minutes per side. Serve immediately.

TOMATO-APRICOT CHUTNEY

You wouldn't think this savory-spicy-sweet chutney would marry well with a basil pesto in a grilled cheese sandwich. I certainly didn't think it would, but I tried it anyway, and the result amazed me. This is a versatile chutney that would also enliven all sorts of foods, from broiled fish to grilled pork chops.

MAKES 3 ½ CUPS

- 1 tablespoon olive oil
- 1 tablespoon finely chopped peeled fresh ginger
- ½ small jalapeño chile, seeded, finely chopped
- 1 teaspoon minced garlic
- 1 tablespoon sugar
- 1 teaspoon brown mustard seeds
- ½ teaspoon ground cumin
- ½ teaspoon fennel seeds
- 1½ cups dried apricots, quartered
- 1 28-ounce can diced tomatoes, juices strained and reserved

Heat the oil in a heavy large saucepan over medium heat. Add the ginger, jalapeño chile, and garlic and sauté until tender, about 2 minutes. Stir in the sugar, mustard seeds, cumin, and fennel seeds and sauté until fragrant, about 1 minute. Stir in the apricots and 6 tablespoons of the reserved tomato juices. Simmer over medium-low heat until the apricots begin to soften, about 5 minutes. Stir in the strained tomatoes. Cover and cook until the tomatoes soften, about 5 minutes.

DO AHEAD: The chutney can be made 3 days ahead. Cool completely. Cover and refrigerate.

continued on next page

BASIL-PARSLEY PESTO

A bit of fresh parsley—flat-leaf or curly—gives this pesto an added dimension of flavor. According to food scientist Harold McGee, flat-leaf parsley has a strong parsley flavor when young and develops a woody flavor when it matures. Curly parsley, on the other hand, is mild when young, developing its stronger parsley flavor as it grows. So choose whichever suits your taste buds.

MAKES ABOUT 2¼ CUPS

1	cup pine nuts
1½	cups (lightly packed) fresh basil leaves (about 1¼ ounces)
½	cup (lightly packed) fresh parsley leaves (about ½ ounce)
4	large garlic cloves, peeled
1	cup high-quality extra-virgin olive oil
1½	cups freshly grated Parmesan cheese (about 5¼ ounces)
½	teaspoon salt
½	teaspoon freshly ground black pepper

Preheat the oven to 350°F. Place the pine nuts on a heavy baking sheet and roast until the pine nuts are golden brown and fragrant, about 8 minutes. Gently shake the baking sheet once or twice as the nuts roast to help ensure they brown evenly. Cool the pine nuts completely.

Combine the pine nuts, basil, parsley, and garlic in a food processor and pulse just until the mixture is finely chopped. With the machine running, gradually blend in the oil. Add the cheese, salt, and pepper and pulse until well blended. Transfer the pesto to a bowl and press plastic wrap directly on to the surface of the pesto to prevent it from discoloring.

DO AHEAD: The pesto can be made up to 3 days ahead, then kept covered and refrigerated.

WARM FILET *of* BEEF SANDWICH *with* CARAMELIZED ONIONS, GORGONZOLA CREAM, *and* ARUGULA *on* SEEDED SOURDOUGH

The beef tenderloin is the cut of the cow that filet mignon steaks come from, so the meat is quite tender and should be cooked rare to medium-rare. Feel free to make extra caramelized onions to use later—they're wonderful in grilled Gruyère cheese sandwiches or piled atop burgers.

~ MAKES 4 SANDWICHES ~

CARAMELIZED ONIONS:

- 3 tablespoons butter
- 2 red onions, peeled and thinly sliced into rings
- ¼ cup red wine vinegar
- ¼ cup sugar
  Salt and freshly ground black pepper

GORGONZOLA CREAM:

- 1½ cups (about 7 ounces) crumbled Gorgonzola cheese
- 3 tablespoons mayonnaise
- 3 tablespoons sour cream

SANDWICHES:

- 1 1¼–pound trimmed center-cut beef tenderloin roast
  Salt and freshly ground black pepper
- 3 tablespoons olive oil, divided
- 8 slices (each about 6 x 3 x ½ inch) seeded sourdough bread
- 2 cups fresh arugula
- 2 tablespoons (¼ stick) butter

TO MAKE THE CARAMELIZED ONIONS: Melt the butter in a heavy large sauté pan over medium heat. Add the onions and sauté until golden brown, about 25 minutes. Add the vinegar and sugar and simmer uncovered over medium-low heat until the liquid evaporates and the onions caramelize, about 5 minutes. Season to taste with salt and pepper. Set aside and keep warm.

MEANWHILE, TO MAKE THE GORGONZOLA CREAM: Blend all the ingredients in a food processor until almost smooth.

DO AHEAD: The caramelized onions and Gorgonzola cream can be made up to 2 days ahead. Cover separately and refrigerate. Rewarm the caramelized onions before using them.

TO ASSEMBLE THE SANDWICHES: Preheat the oven to 350°F. Sprinkle the beef with salt and pepper. Heat 1 tablespoon of oil in a heavy small ovenproof sauté pan over medium heat. Add the beef and cook until brown on all sides, about 10 minutes. Transfer the pan to the oven and roast the beef until an instant-read meat thermometer registers 120°F when inserted into the center of the beef, about 10 minutes. Transfer the beef to a carving board and let rest for 5 minutes. Cut the beef against the grain into thin slices.

Spread the Gorgonzola cream over 1 side of each slice of bread, dividing equally. Place the caramelized onions over 4 bread slices, dividing equally. Arrange the beef slices over the onions. Top with the arugula, then with the remaining bread slices, Gorgonzola cream side down.

Heat 1 tablespoon of oil and 1 tablespoon of butter in a heavy large sauté pan over medium heat. Grill 2 sandwiches until the bread is golden brown and the sandwiches are heated through, about 3 minutes per side. Transfer the sandwiches to a cutting board. Repeat with the remaining 1 tablespoon of oil, 1 tablespoon of butter, and 2 sandwiches. Cut the sandwiches in half and serve warm.

BOURRIDE *with* GRILLED VEGETABLES *and* SAFFRON AÏOLI

I love this slow-cooked French soup, a close cousin to bouillabaisse. It brings back warm memories of the time my daughter Lesley and I took cooking classes in the south of France. We both cherish those days of going to the farmers' market in the morning, cooking together, playing boule and sipping pastis in the late afternoon, and then gathering with friends around the communal table in the evening for our bourride. A good life indeed.

Gather some people you love to share this soup, and serve it with platters of grilled or roasted vegetables, as well as extra aïoli and croutons. I like to accompany it with a salad of garden greens with chèvre, and serve a seasonal fruit croustade for dessert.

~ SERVES 6 ~

CROUTONS:

- 1 small French baguette, cut on sharp diagonal into ¼-inch-thick slices
- 2 tablespoons olive oil
  Salt and freshly ground black pepper

SOUP:

- 2 tablespoons olive oil
- 2 pounds uncooked large shrimp, shelled and deveined, reserving shells
- 4 leeks (white and pale green parts only), sliced
- 4 celery stalks, sliced
- 3 carrots, sliced
- 1 fennel bulb, sliced
- 3 garlic cloves, coarsely chopped
- ⅓ cup tomato paste
- 1½ cups dry white wine
- 8 cups water
- 4 large sprigs thyme
- 3 3 x 1-inch strips orange peel
- ½ teaspoon saffron threads
- ¼ cup Pernod
  Salt and freshly ground black pepper
- 6 ¾-inch-thick slices boneless cod (about 1 pound total)
  Saffron Aïoli (see following recipe)
- 2 extra-large egg yolks
  Grilled Potatoes, Fennel, and Baby Zucchini (see following recipe)

TO MAKE THE CROUTONS: Preheat the oven to 400°F. Brush the baguette slices with the oil. Arrange the baguette slices in a single layer on a rimmed baking sheet and sprinkle with salt and pepper. Bake until golden brown, about 10 minutes.

MEANWHILE, TO MAKE THE SOUP: Heat the oil in a large pot over medium-high heat. Add the shrimp shells, leeks, celery, carrots, fennel, and garlic and sauté until the vegetables soften, about 12 minutes. Stir in the tomato paste, then stir in the wine and the water. Add the thyme, orange peel, and saffron. Bring to a boil, then reduce the heat to medium-low and simmer gently, uncovered, for 45 minutes. Strain the stock through a fine-meshed sieve and into another large wide pot, pressing on the solids to extract as much liquid as possible. Discard the solids. You should have about 6 cups of stock.

DO AHEAD: The croutons and the stock can be made 1 day ahead. Store the croutons in an airtight container at room temperature. Cover and refrigerate the stock.

Stir the Pernod into the stock. Bring the stock to a simmer over medium heat, then reduce the heat to medium-low. Season the stock to taste with salt and pepper. Add the cod and simmer very gently just until it is opaque in the center, about 2 minutes. Using a slotted spoon, place the cod on a platter and tent with foil to keep warm. Add the shrimp to the stock and simmer until the shrimp are just cooked through, about 3 minutes. Using a slotted spoon, transfer the shrimp to the platter with the cod and cover to keep warm.

Gradually whisk ½ cup of the broth into ½ cup of the

continued on next page

aïoli in a medium bowl to blend, then whisk in the egg yolks. Whisk in 1 more cup of the broth. Gradually return the yolk-aïoli mixture to the remaining broth in the pot. Whisk the soup constantly over medium-low heat until the soup thickens slightly, about 5 minutes (do not allow the soup to boil or it will curdle).

Divide the cod and shrimp among 6 large wide soup bowls. Ladle the hot broth over the fish. Spread some of the remaining aïoli over 6 croutons, then set 1 crouton in each bowl of soup. Serve with the grilled vegetables, and the remaining aïoli and croutons alongside so guests can add them to their soup as desired.

SAFFRON AÏOLI

A teaspoon of saffron gives this aïoli a bright yellow color and a wonderful aroma and flavor that complement the bourride perfectly. Note that the oil must be added very slowly to ensure that the mixture remains smooth and creamy. If you're not sure how slowly to pour in the oil, add just ½ teaspoon of oil at a time.

MAKES ABOUT 1⅓ CUPS

- 1 ½-inch-thick slice French bread (about 1 ounce), crust removed
- ¼ cup whole milk
- 3 garlic cloves, peeled
- 2 extra-large egg yolks
- 2 tablespoons fresh lemon juice
- 1 teaspoon saffron threads
- 1 cup extra-virgin olive oil
- ½ teaspoon salt

Tear the bread into small pieces and toss them in a small bowl with the milk. Let stand until the bread becomes soggy, about 5 minutes. Squeeze the bread pieces to exude the excess milk.

Meanwhile, mince the garlic in the food processor. Add the soaked bread, egg yolks, lemon juice, and saffron and process to blend well. With the machine running, slowly add the oil in a thin steady stream, blending until the aïoli becomes thick and creamy. Mix in the salt.

DO AHEAD: The aïoli can be made 2 days ahead. Cover and refrigerate. Whisk the aïoli until smooth and creamy before serving or using.

GRILLED POTATOES, FENNEL, AND BABY ZUCCHINI

Grilled vegetables are a Mediterranean staple and an ideal accompaniment to so many main courses. If you don't have a grill pan or barbecue, you can broil the vegetables instead—arrange them on a baking sheet, making sure they're not crowded, and broil them in batches.

SERVES 6

- 6 small (about 2-inch-diameter) red-skinned potatoes (about 1 pound)
- 1 large fennel bulb, stalks discarded, bulb quartered lengthwise into 4 wedges
- 2 tablespoons plus 2 teaspoons olive oil, divided
  Salt and freshly ground black pepper

Place the potatoes in a large saucepan of salted water. Cook over high heat until the water boils and just until a skewer can slide through a potato without much resistance, about 25 minutes. Drain and set the potatoes on a baking sheet. Set aside to cool completely then cut the potatoes in half.

Meanwhile, preheat a grill pan over medium-high heat or prepare a barbecue for medium-high heat.

Slice the fennel bulb quarters through the core into ¼-inch-thick slices. Lay the fennel slices in a single layer on another baking sheet. Brush 1 tablespoon of the oil over the fennel and sprinkle with salt and pepper. Grill the fennel slices until crisp-tender and grill marks appear, about 3 minutes per side. Transfer the fennel slices to a platter.

Toss the zucchini in a bowl with 2 teaspoons of oil. Sprinkle with salt and pepper. Grill the zucchini until tender and slightly charred, about 3 minutes per side. Transfer the zucchini to the platter with the fennel.

Toss the potatoes in the bowl with the remaining 1 tablespoon of oil. Sprinkle with salt and pepper. Grill the potatoes until golden brown and cooked through, turning to grill all sides, about 5 minutes. Cut the potato halves in half again. Transfer the potatoes to the platter with the fennel and zucchini and serve.

CHOPPED SALAD *with* ROAST CHICKEN *and* VEGETABLES *and* BASIL-PARSLEY PESTO

What makes this a standout in the crowded field of chopped salads are the warm vegetables and the use of pesto instead of a conventional vinaigrette.

~ SERVES 6 ~

3	boneless chicken breasts with skin
8	teaspoons olive oil, divided
	Salt and freshly ground black pepper
2	cups fresh yellow corn kernels (from 3 ears)
1	large zucchini, trimmed, cut into 1-inch cubes
12	asparagus spears, trimmed, cut diagonally into 2-inch pieces
8	cups coarsely chopped romaine lettuce
2	cups finely chopped radicchio
1	cup Basil-Parsley Pesto (page 32)
⅓	cup finely diced red bell pepper, for garnish

Preheat the oven to 475°F. Place the chicken skin side up on a baking sheet. Brush with 2 teaspoons of the oil and sprinkle with salt and pepper. Toss the corn with 2 teaspoons of the oil on another baking sheet to coat and sprinkle with salt and pepper. Roast the chicken until it is just cooked through and golden brown, about 15 minutes. Roast the corn until it is slightly charred and heated through, about 10 minutes. Cut the chicken into 1-inch pieces. Combine the roasted corn and chicken pieces in a large bowl.

Meanwhile, heat 2 teaspoons of the oil in a large sauté pan over high heat. Add the zucchini and sauté until crisp-tender and golden, about 5 minutes. Transfer the zucchini to a large bowl. Heat the remaining 2 teaspoons of oil in the same sauté pan over high heat. Add the asparagus and sauté until crisp-tender and bright green, about 3 minutes. Transfer to the bowl with the zucchini. Add the chicken, corn kernels, romaine lettuce, and radicchio and toss with enough pesto to coat. Season the salad to taste with salt and pepper. Mound the salad on plates. Garnish with the diced red bell pepper and serve.

GRILLED SHRIMP, ASPARAGUS *and* BUTTER LETTUCE SALAD *with* MANGO-PAPAYA SALSA *and* VANILLA BEAN VINAIGRETTE

This is a very pretty salad that's perfect for an elegant luncheon; it's best served plated. The unexpected addition of vanilla bean to the vinaigrette lends a rich, appealing flavor, and the orange juice and zest further bring out the vanilla.

~ SERVES 6 ~

VANILLA BEAN VINAIGRETTE:

- ¼ cup rice wine vinegar
- 3 tablespoons freshly squeezed orange juice
- 1 tablespoon freshly squeezed lemon juice
- 1½ teaspoons finely grated lemon zest
- 1½ teaspoons finely grated orange zest
- ½ teaspoon freshly ground black pepper
- 2 vanilla beans, split lengthwise
- ½ cup olive oil
- ¼ cup canola oil
  Salt

SALAD:

- 30 jumbo shrimp, peeled and deveined
- 2 tablespoons plus 2 teaspoons olive oil, divided
  Salt and freshly ground black pepper
- 24 medium asparagus spears, trimmed
- 30 butter lettuce leaves
  (preferably the mid to center leaves)
  Mango-Papaya Salsa (see following recipe)

FOR THE VANILLA BEAN VINAIGRETTE: Combine the vinegar, orange juice, lemon juice, lemon zest, orange zest, and pepper in a blender. Scrape the seeds from the vanilla beans into the vinegar mixture. Reserve the vanilla beans, if desired. With the blender running, gradually blend in the olive oil and canola oil. Season the vinaigrette to taste with salt. If you're not using the vinaigrette right away, add the vanilla beans to the vinaigrette and let them steep to infuse more vanilla flavor.

DO AHEAD: The vinaigrette can be made 2 days ahead, then kept covered and refrigerated. Whisk before using.

FOR THE SALAD: Preheat a grill pan or prepare a barbecue for medium-high heat. Toss the shrimp in a large bowl with 2 tablespoons of the oil and sprinkle with salt and pepper. Place the asparagus on a baking sheet and brush them with the remaining 2 teaspoons of oil. Sprinkle the asparagus with salt and pepper.

Grill the asparagus until crisp-tender and slightly charred on the outside, about 8 minutes. Grill the shrimp until just cooked through and opaque, about 2 minutes per side.

Place 5 lettuce leaves on each plate. Arrange the shrimp and asparagus spears over the salad. Mound the salsa in the center. Drizzle with the vanilla bean vinaigrette and serve.

MANGO-PAPAYA SALSA

This salsa greatly relies on sweet, ripe, but firm mango and papaya. If you can't find either (or even both) of them, pineapple makes a good substitute.

MAKES 2 CUPS

- 1 small mango, peeled, pitted, and cut into ⅓-inch cubes (about ¾ cup)
- ½ papaya, peeled, seeded, and cut into ⅓-inch cubes (about ¾ cup)
- ⅓ cup finely diced red onion
- ¼ cup coarsely chopped fresh cilantro
- ¼ cup finely diced seeded red bell pepper
- 2 tablespoons fresh lime juice
- 1 tablespoon minced peeled fresh ginger
- 1 tablespoon olive oil
- 2 teaspoons minced seeded jalapeño chile
  Salt

Gently stir all the ingredients in a large bowl, seasoning the salsa to taste with salt.

DO AHEAD: The salsa can be made up to 1 day ahead. Cover and refrigerate.

PARMESAN-CRUSTED SWORDFISH
with LEMON *and* CRISPY CAPER SAUCE

When I'm experimenting in the kitchen, I try to stay open-minded and ignore culinary traditions. This dish resulted from flauting the old rule about not pairing fish and cheese. I introduced this dish as a special, and it was such a hit that it entered the regular menu, remaining a customer favorite to this day. The creamy, tangy sauce and crispy capers complement both the Parmesan crust and the fish. If you can't get good swordfish, chicken works well. Note that the sauce can be tossed with pasta or served with any other fish—and the deep-fried capers are just as versatile.

~ SERVES 6 ~

SAUCE AND FRIED CAPERS:

- 2 cups dry vermouth
- 2 shallots, minced
- 1 cup heavy cream
- 2 tablespoons plus ¼ cup drained capers, divided
- 1½ tablespoons fresh lemon juice
- 1 tablespoon finely chopped fresh chives
- 1 garlic clove, minced
  Salt and freshly ground black pepper
  Canola oil, for frying

SWORDFISH:

- 1¼ cups unbleached all-purpose flour, divided
- 2½ teaspoons salt, plus more to taste
- 1 teaspoon freshly ground black pepper, plus more to taste
- 1 cup finely grated Parmesan cheese
- 1½ tablespoons minced garlic
- 1 tablespoon minced fresh parsley
- 1 cup heavy cream
- 2 extra-large eggs
- 6 6-ounce swordfish steaks (each about ¾ inch thick)
- 2 tablespoons (¼ stick) butter
- 4 tablespoons olive oil
  Minced fresh chives, for garnish

TO PREPARE THE SAUCE: Combine the vermouth and shallots in a heavy medium saucepan and simmer over high heat until it is reduced to 1 cup, about 30 minutes. Add the cream and simmer until the sauce thickens and reduces slightly, about 5 minutes longer. Strain the sauce into a small saucepan. Stir in 2 tablespoons of the capers, and the lemon juice, chives, and garlic. Season the sauce to taste with salt and pepper. Cover the sauce and keep it warm.

MEANWHILE, TO FRY THE CAPERS: Pour enough canola oil into a small saucepan to reach a depth of 1 inch. Heat the oil over medium-high heat. Add the remaining ¼ cup of capers and fry until they puff and become crisp, about 1 minute. Using a slotted spoon, transfer the fried capers to paper towels to drain any excess oil.

TO PREPARE THE SWORDFISH: Mix 1 cup of flour, 2 teaspoons of salt, and 1 teaspoon of pepper to blend in a pie pan or shallow dish. Mix the Parmesan cheese, garlic, parsley, remaining ¼ cup of flour, and remaining ½ teaspoon of salt in another pie pan to blend. Lastly, whisk the cream and eggs in a third shallow pie pan to blend.

Dredge the swordfish in the seasoned flour to coat lightly and completely. Shake off the excess flour, then dip the swordfish into the egg mixture to coat completely. Lift the swordfish and allow the excess egg mixture to drip off. Lastly, coat the swordfish completely with the Parmesan mixture, patting to adhere. Transfer the coated swordfish to a baking sheet.

DO AHEAD: The sauce, fried capers, and coated swordfish can be made up to 1 day ahead. After the sauce is strained, cover and refrigerate it, then rewarm it over medium-high heat before adding the drained capers, lemon juice, chives, and garlic. Cover the fried capers and keep them at room temperature. Cover and refrigerate the coated swordfish.

Melt 1 tablespoon of butter with 2 tablespoons of oil in each of 2 heavy large frying pans over medium-high heat. Add 3 coated swordfish to each pan and cook until golden brown on the bottom, about 3 minutes. Using a metal spatula, turn the fish over and cook until they are opaque in the center and golden brown on the bottom, about 2 minutes.

Transfer the swordfish to plates. Spoon the sauce over and sprinkle with the fried capers and chives.

Gourmet Market

SOUPS

Carrot with Ginger *51*

Roasted Red Pepper and Pear *52*

Fresh Pea with Mint *53*

Cabbage, Apple and Thyme *55*

Roasted Corn and Cilantro Chowder *56*

SIDES / SALADS

Lemon-Herb Roasted Chicken
in a Bread Basket *57*

Wild Rice, Dried Apricots and Toasted
Pecan Salad with Port Vinaigrette *59*

Orzo, Salad with Feta,
Mint and Green Onions *61*

Linguini Chinois *62*

Roasted Potato Salad with Snow Peas,
Parmesan, Lemon and Garlic *63*

Lentil Salad with Currants
and Turmeric Vinaigrette *65*

Celery Root, Apple and Radish Salad
with Mustard Seed Vinaigrette *67*

Red Cabbage Slaw with Toasted
Walnuts and Gorgonzola *68*

ENTREES

Beef Daube Provençal *69*

Salmon with Pistachio
and Dried Cranberry Crust
Orange-Chipotle Vinaigrette *71*

Chicken Strips with
Ginger-Apricot Sauce *72*

Tomato, Basil Pesto and
Three-Cheese Strata *75*

Chicken and Mushroom Bread Pudding
with Tarragon and Gruyère Cheese *76*

Baby Back Pork Ribs with Espresso
Barbecue Glaze *77*

Chicken Breasts
with Cherry-Rhubarb Chutney *79*

PASTRIES

Blackberry Polenta Bread Pudding *81*

Lemon Soufflé Pudding Cake *82*

Hummingbird Cake with Banana,
Pineapple and Pecans *83*

Apple Pie Cake
with Whiskey Caramel Sauce *85*

Spiced Pumpkin Cheesecake
with Gingersnap Crust *86*

Sugar-Crusted Nectarine, Blueberry
and Toasted Almond Croustades *89*

Lemon Coconut Bars *90*

Graham Cracker Chewy Bars *91*

Crystallized Ginger Cookies *93*

Chocolate Espresso Cream Cheese Bars *94*

My business started with just me and a home kitchen. But when I moved into the restaurant space on Mission Street, I had to hire help, and very quickly the business became so much more than me. Words cannot describe the depth of affection and gratitude I have for the Julienne staff, some of whom have worked with me for many, many years. Our employees are our biggest asset—they take care of our customers and make them feel at home. I couldn't do any of this without them.

Chief among these people is my partner and daughter Julie Campoy, who joined me in 1989 and immediately set to work on growing the Gourmet Market. She saw the trend that was just about to hit: an increasing number of working women and two-income couples who cared about eating well but worked long hours and couldn't spend the afternoon cooking. Further complicating family life was the increase in after-school sports and activities that often interfered with a proper sit-down dinner, which I consider so essential to the fabric of family life. So we started doing the cooking for them, and I'm glad for our part in helping families eat together. In fact, a great many of these customers have come to see Julienne as an extension of their home kitchen, and many of them come every day, to have lunch, pick up something for dinner, or get cookies for a school function.

It took time and some trial and error to learn what our customers wanted and to give it to them in our own way. At first, I felt that frozen food would not do well, so we had a small selection. Julie, however, thought our customers would respond to frozen, ready-to-go dishes, and indeed they did—people would come in and buy a week's worth of entrees at a time, emptying our freezers. So when we remodeled in 1992, we added two more freezers and came up with a variety of things to fill them with, from soups to stratas, casseroles to cookie dough. Some of our freezer staples today, like the beef daube, are classics that have been in demand from the beginning.

The freezer is but one corner of the market. Elsewhere are deli cases filled with salads, ready-to-go entrees, and baked goods, and a self-serve refrigerated section stocked with sauces, chutneys, vinaigrettes, condiments, cheeses, and individual salads, sandwiches, and entrees. As more people came in to pick up prepared foods, Julie continued to grow the market, and now our regulars shop here for cookbooks, tabletop décor, hostess gifts, and specialty foods. We expanded by listening to our customers, many of whom have become our friends—when they started asking for wine, or boxed lunches, or roasted turkeys, or freezer food shipped out of state, we took care of them. Perhaps the biggest part of our market business today is one we didn't expect: takeout celebrations, from office lunches and Hollywood Bowl box dinners to multicourse holiday dinners and parties for a few hundred. One of the reasons our customers are so loyal is because they appreciate that we make every single thing from scratch, from our signature rosemary-currant bread to our vinaigrettes, chutneys, and sauces.

The beauty of freezer food is that the overscheduled home cook can still create richly flavorful meals in advance. For instance, the Roasted Corn and Cilantro Chowder, Carrot Ginger Soup, Beef Daube Provençal, and Spiced Pumpkin Cheesecake with Gingersnap Crust all freeze beautifully. Other dishes in this chapter, from Linguine Chinois to Wild Rice, Dried Apricots and Toasted Pecan Salad with Port Vinaigrette, are easy to make ahead and store in the refrigerator. We are particularly proud of our salads, which fill our deli case every day. And then there are the desserts, my first love and still a cornerstone of our market business.

These and all the other dishes you'll discover in this chapter work well for both family meals and casual parties; many make terrific contributions to a potluck. Each earned its spot in these pages the hard way: after years of being made in our kitchen, because our customers kept asking for them. They're all classics, blending traditional home cooking with a respect for good ingredients and a modern sensibility, and they're all likely to become best sellers in your house, too.

CARROT GINGER SOUP

Carrots are the single most important ingredient in this recipe, so be sure to use the freshest ones you can find. Look for some with their feathery green tops intact, which is a sign of freshness. Chopped toasted pecans and grated crystallized ginger make a pretty garnish for this velvety soup.

~ SERVES 4 TO 6 ~

2	tablespoons olive oil
1	pound carrots, peeled, grated
1	large leek (white and pale green parts only), chopped
3	tablespoons finely chopped peeled fresh ginger
4	teaspoons finely grated orange zest
6	cups chicken stock or vegetable stock
½	cup fresh orange juice
3	tablespoons finely chopped crystallized ginger
½	teaspoon salt, plus more to taste
¼	teaspoon freshly ground black pepper, plus more to taste
2	tablespoons (¼ stick) unsalted butter

Heat the oil in a heavy large pot over medium heat. Add the carrots, leeks, fresh ginger, and orange zest. Sauté until the leeks are translucent and the carrots soften, about 10 minutes. Add the stock, orange juice, crystallized ginger, ½ teaspoon of salt, and ¼ teaspoon of pepper. Bring to a simmer over high heat, then reduce the heat to medium-low. Simmer uncovered until the vegetables are tender, stirring occasionally, about 15 minutes. Cool slightly.

Working in batches, transfer the soup to a blender and puree until very smooth. Transfer the pureed soup to a clean large saucepan and return to a simmer over low heat. Remove the soup from the heat and whisk in the butter. Season the soup to taste with salt and pepper.

DO AHEAD: The soup can be made 1 day ahead. Cool completely, then cover and refrigerate. Rewarm, covered, over medium heat, stirring occasionally.

ROASTED RED PEPPER *and* PEAR SOUP

This is one of my favorite soups, because the flavors are so unexpected and the color is so bright. Pears and peppers may not seem like a natural pairing, but the rich sweetness of the pear balances the acidity of the peppers, resulting in smoothly delicious soup. Garnish with finely diced pears or a chiffonade of mildly flavored fresh herbs, such as tarragon or marjoram.

~ SERVES 6 ~

12	medium red bell peppers (about 3 pounds total), halved, seeded, divided
3	tablespoons unsalted butter
3	tablespoons olive oil
3	carrots, peeled, thinly sliced
2	Bosc pears, peeled, thinly sliced
3	shallots, thinly sliced
2	garlic cloves, thinly sliced
6	cups chicken stock
2	tablespoons canned diced green chiles
1	tablespoon chopped fresh tarragon
1½	teaspoons salt, plus more to taste
½	teaspoon freshly ground black pepper, plus more to taste

Preheat the oven to 500°F. Arrange 6 of the red bell peppers on a heavy large baking sheet and roast them in the oven until they are tender and slightly charred, turning them once, about 25 minutes. Enclose the peppers in a plastic bag and set them aside until they are cool enough to handle. Peel and seed the roasted peppers, then set them aside.

Meanwhile, thinly slice the remaining 6 bell peppers. Melt the butter with the oil in a heavy large pot over medium-high heat. Add the sliced peppers, carrots, pears, shallots, and garlic and sauté until the peppers are very tender and the shallots just begin to brown, about 25 minutes. Add the chicken stock, green chiles, tarragon, 1½ teaspoons of salt, and ½ teaspoon of black pepper. Bring to a simmer, then reduce the heat to medium-low. Cover and simmer gently to allow the flavors to blend, stirring occasionally, about 25 minutes. Cool slightly.

Working in batches, transfer the soup and reserved roasted bell peppers to a food processor and puree until smooth. Strain the soup into another pot and return the soup to a simmer over low heat. Season to taste with salt and pepper. Ladle the soup into bowls and serve.

DO AHEAD: The soup can be made 1 day ahead. Cool completely, then cover and refrigerate. Rewarm, covered, over medium heat, stirring occasionally.

FRESH PEA SOUP *with* MINT

In my catering days, we often served this soup chilled at ladies' luncheons, garnishing it with such edible flowers as pansies or nasturtiums. Today, we love the idea of serving it either warm or cool in demitasse cups as an amuse-bouche, or tray-passed as an hors d'oeurve.

~ SERVES 6 TO 8 ~

3	tablespoons unsalted butter
2	tablespoons olive oil
3	leeks (about 12 ounces total; white and pale green parts only), chopped
10	shallots (about 11 ounces total), thinly sliced
3¾	pounds fresh petite green peas (about 12 cups) or frozen, thawed
4	cups chicken stock
3	tablespoons finely chopped fresh mint leaves
1	teaspoon salt, plus more to taste
¼	teaspoon freshly ground white pepper, plus more to taste
	Fresh mint leaves, very thinly sliced (chiffonade), for garnish

Melt the butter with the oil in a heavy medium pot over medium-high heat. Add the leeks and shallots and sauté until soft, about 5 minutes. Stir in the peas. Add the stock, chopped mint, 1 teaspoon of salt, and ¼ teaspoon of white pepper. Simmer until the peas are tender, stirring occasionally, about 12 minutes. Cool slightly.

Working in batches, transfer the soup to a blender and puree until smooth. Strain the soup into another pot; discard the solids. Return the soup to a simmer over low heat. Season the soup to taste with more salt and white pepper. Ladle the soup into bowls, garnish with the mint chiffonade and serve.

DO AHEAD: The soup can be made 1 day ahead. Cool completely, then cover and refrigerate. Rewarm, covered, over medium heat, stirring occasionally.

CABBAGE, APPLE *and* THYME SOUP

This soup reminds me of French onion soup—it's both sweet and savory, and it has a wonderful cheese topping. Cabbage replaces some of the onion, and the caramelized apples add sweetness. When paired with a salad, this soup makes a comforting light supper. It also makes a lovely first course for a seated dinner party.

~ SERVES 6 ~

2	tablespoons olive oil
8	cups thinly sliced green cabbage (from 1 head)
1	large onion, chopped
1	tablespoon minced fresh thyme
1½	teaspoons salt, plus more to taste
1	teaspoon freshly ground black pepper, plus more to taste
6	cups chicken broth
2	tablespoons (¼ stick) unsalted butter
1½	pounds Fuji apples, peeled, cored, cut into ½-inch cubes
2	cups (lightly packed; about 8 ounces) grated Gruyère cheese

Heat the oil in a heavy large pot over medium-high heat. Add the cabbage and onions and sauté until the vegetables are soft and pale golden brown, about 15 minutes. Stir in the thyme, 1½ teaspoons of salt, and 1 teaspoon of pepper. Add the broth and bring to a boil. Reduce the heat to medium-low and simmer for 10 minutes.

Meanwhile, melt the butter in a heavy large skillet over medium-high heat. Add the apples and sauté until brown and tender, about 12 minutes. Add the apples to the soup. Simmer gently over medium-low heat for about 5 minutes to allow the flavors to blend. Season to taste with more salt and pepper, if desired.

DO AHEAD: The soup can be made up to this point 1 day ahead. Cool completely, then cover and refrigerate. Rewarm, covered, over medium heat, stirring occasionally.

Preheat the broiler. Ladle the soup into 6 flameproof bowls. Sprinkle the cheese over the soup. Set the bowls on a heavy baking sheet and broil until the cheese melts, about 1 minute.

ROASTED CORN *and* CILANTRO CHOWDER

This chunky chowder is hearty and filling, well worthy of a simple supper. Thanks to our talented kitchen staff, such Latin staples as cilantro and green chiles have made their way into many of our dishes, including this chowder. If you'd prefer a more traditional chowder, just leave out the cilantro and chiles—or replace the chiles with diced red bell peppers and use a bit of fresh chopped parsley instead of cilantro. There's no harm in tossing in some cooked bacon, either!

~ **SERVES 6 TO 8** ~

6	cups (about 2 pounds) frozen yellow corn kernels, thawed, divided
1	tablespoon olive oil
1	tablespoon salt, plus more to taste
1	teaspoon freshly ground black pepper, plus more to taste
5	tablespoons unsalted butter
4	leeks (white and pale green parts only), minced
1	onion, minced
3	celery ribs, minced
6	cups chicken stock
1	cup heavy cream
½	cup canned diced green chiles
¼	teaspoon dried hot red pepper flakes, plus more to taste
2	pounds russet potatoes (about 2 large), peeled, cut into ½-inch cubes
1	cup coarsely chopped fresh cilantro (from 2 bunches)

Preheat the oven to 500°F. Toss 3 cups of the corn on a heavy baking sheet with the oil to coat. Season with salt and pepper. Roast until the corn is golden brown, stirring occasionally, about 25 minutes.

Meanwhile, melt the butter in a heavy large pot over medium heat. Add the leeks, onions, and celery. Sauté until the vegetables are soft and the onions are translucent, about 15 minutes. Add the chicken stock, cream, chilies, ¼ teaspoon of red pepper flakes, remaining 3 cups of corn, 1 tablespoon of salt, and 1 teaspoon of black pepper. Bring to a simmer over medium-high heat. Add the potatoes and cilantro and simmer uncovered over medium-low heat until the potatoes are almost tender, stirring occasionally, about 15 minutes. Add the roasted corn and continue simmering until the potatoes are tender, about 5 minutes longer. Season the chowder to taste with more salt, black pepper, and pepper flakes. Ladle the chowder into bowls and serve.

DO AHEAD: The chowder can be made 1 day ahead. Cool completely, then cover and refrigerate. Rewarm, covered, over medium heat, stirring occasionally.

LEMON-HERB ROASTED CHICKEN *in a* BREAD BASKET

In my early days as a caterer, I'd make this for my friends, who would pick it up from my house to take to the Hollywood Bowl. It's great fun for any picnic: everyone gets a piece of chicken and takes part in tearing and eating the edible garlicky bread bowl. Look for a large round loaf of country-style bread (known as a boule), and if the chicken breasts are very large, cut them in half.

~ SERVES 4 ~

- 2   boneless chicken breasts (with skin)
- 2   chicken legs
- 2   chicken thighs (with skin and bones)
-     Salt and freshly ground black pepper
- 2   tablespoons olive oil
- 1   tablespoon finely chopped fresh rosemary
- 1   tablespoon lemon zest
- 6   garlic cloves, minced, divided
- 1   2-pound loaf sourdough bread (about 10 x 7-inch oval and 4½ inches high)
- ½   cup (1 stick) unsalted butter
- ¼   cup chopped fresh parsley

Preheat the oven to 450°F. Sprinkle the chicken breasts, legs, and thighs with salt and pepper. Stir the oil, rosemary, lemon zest, and 2 minced garlic cloves in a small bowl to blend. Spread the mixture all over the chicken. Arrange the chicken on a heavy large rimmed baking sheet and roast until golden brown and just cooked through, about 30 minutes.

Meanwhile, using a serrated knife and starting 1 inch from the edge of the bread, cut off the top. Then cut out the interior of the bread, leaving a 1-inch-thick lining. Melt the butter in a heavy small saucepan over medium heat. Add the remaining 4 minced garlic cloves and the parsley. Spoon the butter mixture over the interior of the bread bowl and the cut side of the bread lid. Sprinkle with salt and pepper.

Reduce the oven temperature to 375°F. Arrange the roast chicken pieces in the bread bowl. Cover with the bread lid. Wrap the bread bowl with foil, encasing completely. Set the bread bowl on a baking sheet and bake until the bread bowl is hot but not crusty, about 20 minutes. Wrap the bread bowl with newspaper and transfer to a picnic basket.

WILD RICE, DRIED APRICOTS *and* TOASTED PECAN SALAD *with* PORT VINAIGRETTE

Port serves double duty in this salad. First, while the apricots, currants, and figs soak in the fortified wine and become plump, they transfer some of their flavors to each other. Second, once the fruit is removed, the flavored Port then becomes part of a luxurious vinaigrette. Garnish the salad with halved figs, whole apricots, and orange zest to let your guests know what's inside.

~ SERVES 8 TO 10 ~

SALAD:

1	cup wild rice
4	cups cold water
½	teaspoon salt
1	cup dried apricots, cut into ⅓-inch pieces
1	cup dried currants
⅔	cup dried figs, cut into ⅓-inch pieces
¾	cup ruby Port
4	celery ribs, diced
5	green onions, thinly sliced
1	red apple, peeled, cored, diced
½	cup seedless green grapes, cut in half
½	cup pecans, toasted, chopped

PORT VINAIGRETTE:

½	cup reserved ruby Port (from soaking dried fruits)
	Zest of 2 oranges (about 2 tablespoons)
	Juice of 1 lemon (about 3 tablespoons)
1	tablespoon balsamic vinegar
¾	teaspoon salt, plus more to taste
½	teaspoon freshly ground black pepper, plus more to taste
½	cup olive oil

TO PREPARE THE SALAD: Wash the rice in a fine-meshed strainer, then place the rice in a bowl. Pour enough boiling water over the rice to cover. Soak for 30 minutes to allow the rice to soften. Drain.

Place the rice in a large saucepan with the cold water and the salt. Bring the water to a boil, then reduce the heat to medium-low. Cover and simmer until the rice is tender but not mushy, about 25 minutes. Drain the excess cooking liquid from the rice and set the rice aside to cool.

Meanwhile, combine the apricots, currants, and figs in a medium bowl. Add the Port and soak for 30 minutes. Drain well and reserve ½ cup of the Port in a medium bowl for the dressing. Combine the soaked fruits, wild rice, celery, green onions, apples, grapes, and pecans in another large bowl.

TO MAKE THE PORT VINAIGRETTE: Mix the reserved Port, orange zest, lemon juice, vinegar, ¾ teaspoon of salt, and ½ teaspoon of pepper in a blender. With the blender running, gradually add the oil and blend well.

Toss the rice mixture with enough vinaigrette to moisten and coat. Season the salad to taste with more salt and pepper, if desired.

DO AHEAD: The salad can be prepared 1 day ahead, then covered and refrigerated. Bring to room temperature and season with more salt and pepper, if desired, before serving.

ORZO SALAD *with* FETA, MINT *and* GREEN ONIONS

Because this is an excellent salad to serve with lamb, it's particularly popular in spring and on Easter buffets. It can be made the day before, and it tastes wonderful and is best served at room temperature.

~ SERVES 8 TO 10 ~

1   pound orzo
3   red bell peppers, seeded, cut into ½-inch dice
3   yellow bell peppers, seeded, cut into ½-inch dice
4   garlic cloves, minced
½   cup olive oil (preferably fruity olive oil), divided
     Salt and freshly ground black pepper
5   green onions, minced
12   ounces feta cheese, coarsely crumbled
½   cup (lightly packed) fresh mint leaves, chopped
⅓   cup pine nuts, lightly toasted
2   tablespoons fresh lemon juice

Cook the orzo in a large saucepan of boiling salted water until just tender, stirring frequently to prevent the orzo from sticking, about 10 minutes. Drain well and transfer to a baking sheet to cool completely.

Meanwhile, preheat the broiler. Toss the peppers and garlic in a large roasting pan with ¼ cup of the olive oil to coat. Season with salt and black pepper. Broil the mixture, stirring occasionally, until soft and lightly blistered, about 20 minutes.

Combine the cooked orzo, broiled vegetables, green onions, feta cheese, mint, and pine nuts in a large bowl. Toss the salad with the lemon juice and enough of the remaining ¼ cup of oil to moisten thoroughly. Season the salad to taste with black pepper.

DO AHEAD: The salad can be made 1 day ahead, then covered and refrigerated. Serve cold or at room temperature.

LINGUINE CHINOIS

This lively pasta salad made its debut when Julienne first opened, and it's been one of our most popular salads ever since. To turn it into a more substantial entrée, simply add a julienne of roasted chicken.

~ SERVES 8 ~

- ¼ cup honey
- 2 tablespoons soy sauce
- 1 teaspoon dried hot red pepper flakes
- ¼ cup toasted sesame oil
- 2 tablespoons corn oil
- 1 pound linguine
- ½ cup chopped fresh cilantro
- ¾ cup sliced green onions
- ½ cup roasted unsalted peanuts, chopped
- 3 tablespoons toasted sesame seeds

Whisk the honey, soy sauce, and red pepper flakes in a small saucepan to blend. Whisk in the sesame oil and corn oil. Stir over low heat until the dressing is warm, about 5 minutes. Set aside and cover to keep warm.

Meanwhile, cook the linguine in a large pot of boiling water until tender, stirring often to prevent the pasta from sticking. Drain well (do not rinse the linguine).

Toss the hot linguine in a large bowl with the warm dressing. Mix in the cilantro, green onions, peanuts, and sesame seeds. Set aside until the linguine cools to room temperature and absorbs the dressing, tossing occasionally. Serve warm, at room temperature, or cold.

DO AHEAD: The salad can be made 1 day ahead, then covered and refrigerated.

ROASTED POTATO SALAD *with* SNOW PEAS, PARMESAN, LEMON *and* GARLIC

The key to this dish is getting the flavors of the olive oil, lemon, and garlic infused into the potatoes so be sure to have the mixture ready, and toss it with the potatoes the moment they come out of the oven. You can use a vegetable peeler to shave the Parmesan into pretty little curls.

~ SERVES 8 ~

2	pounds small (about 2-inch-diameter) red-skinned potatoes
2	cups (about 6 ounces) snow peas, trimmed, strings discarded
5	tablespoons extra-virgin olive oil
4	garlic cloves, minced
2	tablespoons lemon zest
¾	teaspoon kosher salt, plus more to taste
½	teaspoon coarsely ground black pepper, plus more to taste
½	cup 1-inch pieces fresh chives
1	cup shaved Parmesan cheese (about 2¾ ounces), divided

Preheat the oven to 350°F. Pierce each potato 5 or 6 times with a fork. Place the potatoes on a heavy large baking sheet and roast them in the oven until they are tender, about 1 hour. Set the potatoes aside until they are just cool enough to handle.

Meanwhile, cook the snow peas in a large saucepan of boiling salted water until they are bright green and crisp-tender, about 2 minutes. Using a slotted spoon, transfer the snow peas to a large bowl of ice water. Set aside until the snow peas are cold. Drain and pat the snow peas dry with paper towels.

Whisk the olive oil, garlic, lemon zest, ¾ teaspoon of salt, and ½ teaspoon of pepper in a large bowl to blend. Cut the hot potatoes in half, or quarter them if they are large. Immediately add the hot potatoes to the olive oil and lemon zest mixture and toss to coat. Add the snow peas, chives, and half of the cheese and toss again. Season the salad to taste with more salt and pepper, if desired. Scatter the remaining cheese over the salad and serve warm or at room temperature.

DO AHEAD: The salad can be prepared 2 hours ahead. Cover and keep at room temperature.

LENTIL SALAD *with* CURRANTS *and* TURMERIC VINAIGRETTE

Fans of curry love this hearty lentil salad, because the turmeric, coriander, cumin, and other spices in the vinaigrette are redolent of the best curries. It's a vegetarian dish that carnivores like, and it's a great contribution to a potluck.

~ SERVES 10 ~

TURMERIC VINAIGRETTE:
- ½ cup red wine vinegar
- ¼ cup Dijon mustard
- 1 tablespoon turmeric
- 1 teaspoon kosher salt
- ½ teaspoon freshly ground black pepper
- ½ teaspoon ground coriander
- ½ teaspoon ground cumin
- ¼ teaspoon cayenne pepper
- ¼ teaspoon ground cinnamon
- ¼ teaspoon ground cloves
- ¼ teaspoon ground nutmeg
- 1¼ cups canola oil

SALAD:
- 10 cups water
- 3 cups dried lentils
- 2 cups finely chopped red onion
- 1½ cups dried currants
- 1 cup chopped fresh parsley
- ⅓ cup drained capers
- Salt and freshly ground black pepper

TO MAKE THE TURMERIC VINAIGRETTE: Blend all the ingredients except the oil in a blender until smooth. With the blender running, gradually add the oil and blend well.

TO PREPARED THE SALAD: Bring the water to a boil in a large saucepan. Add the lentils and cook for 5 minutes. Turn off the heat and let stand until the lentils are just tender but still firm to the bite, about 20 minutes. Drain well; transfer the lentils to a heavy large rimmed baking sheet and set aside until the lentils are completely cool, stirring occasionally to help the steam dissipate.

Mix the onions, currants, parsley, and capers in a large bowl. Add the lentils and toss well. Toss the salad with enough vinaigrette to coat. Season to taste with salt and black pepper. Let stand, tossing occasionally, to allow the lentils to absorb some of the vinaigrette, about 30 minutes. Serve at room temperature or cover and refrigerate and serve cold.

DO AHEAD: The salad can be made 1 day ahead, then covered and refrigerated. Serve cold or at room temperature.

CELERY ROOT, APPLE *and* RADISH SALAD *with* MUSTARD SEED VINAIGRETTE

I named Julienne in part for the French term that refers to a cut that is about the size of a small matchstick. This is a Julienne recipe that requires you to julienne! If you weren't trained by a French chef to julienne perfectly, not to worry—use a mandoline or other vegetable slicer to quickly cut the vegetables into even little strips.

~ SERVES 8 ~

MUSTARD SEED VINAIGRETTE:

1	shallot, sliced
2	tablespoons coarse Dijon mustard
1½	tablespoons apple cider vinegar
1	tablespoon fresh lemon juice
1	tablespoon honey
1	teaspoon freshly ground black pepper
½	teaspoon salt, plus more to taste
6	tablespoons canola oil
1	tablespoon chopped fresh parsley
1	teaspoon finely chopped fresh tarragon

SALAD:

2	celery roots (about 2¼ pounds total), peeled, julienned
1	green apple, unpeeled, cored, julienned
6	radishes, julienned
½	cup very thinly sliced red onion
2	tablespoons minced fresh parsley

TO MAKE THE MUSTARD SEED VINAIGRETTE: Blend the shallot, mustard, vinegar, lemon juice, honey, pepper, and ½ teaspoon of salt in a blender until smooth. With the machine running, gradually blend in the oil. Blend in the parsley and tarragon. Season the vinaigrette with more salt, if desired. Set the vinaigrette aside.

TO MAKE THE SALAD: Toss the celery root strips and vinaigrette in a large bowl to coat. Cover and refrigerate for 1 hour. Add the apples, radishes, onions, and parsley, and toss to combine.

DO AHEAD: The salad can be made 4 hours ahead, then covered and refrigerated.

RED CABBAGE SLAW *with* TOASTED WALNUTS *and* GORGONZOLA

Cole slaw is a basic at every barbecue, potluck, and picnic. This recipe, however, is anything but basic. The Gorgonzola gives it richness, the toasted walnuts give it elegance, and the Dijon vinaigrette gives it a lively flavor.

~ SERVES 8~

- ¾ cup walnut halves
- ¼ cup extra-virgin olive oil
- 2 tablespoons red wine vinegar
- 1 tablespoon Dijon mustard
- 1 teaspoon ground cumin
- ½ teaspoon kosher salt, plus more to taste
- 6 cups thinly sliced red cabbage (from 1 head)
- ⅓ cup minced fresh parsley
- ¾ cup coarsely crumbled Gorgonzola cheese (about 2½ ounces)
  Freshly ground black pepper

Preheat the oven to 350°F. Place the walnuts on a heavy baking sheet and toast them in the oven until they are fragrant and golden brown in the center, about 10 minutes. Set aside to cool. Coarsely chop the walnuts.

Whisk the oil, vinegar, mustard, cumin, and ½ teaspoon of salt in a medium bowl to blend. Toss the cabbage, parsley, Gorgonzola cheese, and toasted walnuts in a large bowl with enough vinaigrette to coat. Season to taste with more salt and freshly ground black pepper.

DO AHEAD: The salad can be made 4 hours ahead, then covered and refrigerated.

BEEF DAUBE PROVENÇAL

I've been making this daube since my earliest days as a caterer, and to this day it's probably our single most popular dish. A Food Network cooking show once recommended it as one of the best foods to order by FedEx, and every time that episode re-runs, we get inundated with orders. All you need to make this a comforting family meal is a mixed baby greens salad or our Harvest Salad (page 149) and a fresh, warm baguette.

~ SERVES 6 TO 8 ~

6	tablespoons (about) olive oil, divided
2	large onions, chopped
1	tablespoon minced garlic
8	sprigs fresh thyme
2	bay leaves
4	pounds top sirloin, cut into 1½-inch cubes
2	teaspoons salt, plus more for seasoning beef
2	teaspoons freshly ground black pepper, plus more for seasoning beef
4	tablespoons unbleached all-purpose flour
3	cups beef stock
¼	cup tomato paste
¼	cup red currant jelly
3	cups dry red wine
1½	teaspoons finely grated orange zest (from 1 large orange)
1½	pounds large carrots, peeled, cut diagonally into 1-inch pieces
1½	pounds 2-inch-diameter red-skinned potatoes, cut in half
1	cup (about 6 ounces) pearl onions, peeled

Preheat the oven to 350°F. Heat 3 tablespoons of the oil in a heavy large Dutch oven over medium-high heat. Add the chopped onions, garlic, thyme, and bay leaves and sauté until the onions are translucent and very tender, about 8 minutes. Using a slotted spoon, transfer the vegetables to a large bowl and set aside.

Heat 2 tablespoons of the remaining oil in the same pot over medium-high heat. Sprinkle the beef with salt and pepper. Toss half of the beef with 2 tablespoons of flour in a medium bowl to coat lightly. Add the floured beef to the pot and cook until brown on all sides, about 8 minutes. Transfer the beef to the bowl with the onion mixture. Repeat coating the remaining beef with the remaining 2 tablespoons of flour and cooking it until brown, adding more oil to the pot as needed.

Add the beef stock to the pot and stir to scrape up the browned bits on the bottom of the pot. Return all the beef, the sautéed onion mixture, and any accumulated juices from the bowl to the pot. Stir in the tomato paste, currant jelly, and remaining 2 teaspoons of salt and black pepper. Add the wine. Bring the liquid to a simmer. Stir in the orange zest. Add the carrots, potatoes, and pearl onions. Cover the pot and place it in the oven until the beef is very tender and moist, about 2 hours.

DO AHEAD: The daube can be made 1 day ahead. Cool completely, then cover and refrigerate. Rewarm the daube over medium-low heat, covered, stirring occasionally.

SALMON *with* PISTACHIO *and* DRIED CRANBERRY CRUST *and* ORANGE-CHIPOTLE VINAIGRETTE

This dish is popular at Julienne year-round. In the summertime, it's ideal for picnics, because it tastes as good at room temperature as it does hot. In the winter, it's a pretty and festive addition to any holiday buffet, thanks to the red cranberries and green pistachios.

~ SERVES 6 ~

ORANGE-CHIPOTLE VINAIGRETTE:

- 1 cup fresh orange juice
- ⅓ cup olive oil
- 2 tablespoons chopped fresh cilantro
- 2 tablespoons fresh lime juice
- 1 tablespoon grated orange zest
- 2 teaspoons honey
- 1 teaspoon chopped fresh oregano
- 1 teaspoon grated lime zest
- 1 teaspoon ground cumin
- 1 teaspoon minced chipotle chiles in adobo

    Salt

SALMON:

- 2 tablespoons olive oil, divided
- 1 2¾-pound boneless skinless salmon filet

    Salt and freshly ground black pepper
- ½ cup dried cranberries, coarsely chopped
- ½ cup shelled raw pistachio nuts, coarsely chopped

TO PREPARE THE ORANGE-CHIPOTLE VINAIGRETTE: Boil the orange juice in a heavy small saucepan over medium-high heat until reduced to ½ cup, about 8 minutes. Cool completely.

Combine the orange juice reduction, oil, and the remaining vinaigrette ingredients in a blender. Blend until smooth. Season the vinaigrette to taste with salt.

TO PREPARE THE SALMON: Preheat the oven to 425°F. Line a large rimmed baking sheet with foil and generously brush the foil with 1 tablespoon of the oil. Place the salmon, flat side down, on the prepared baking sheet. Coat the salmon with the remaining 1 tablespoon of oil. Sprinkle with salt and pepper. Toss the cranberries and pistachio nuts in a small bowl. Sprinkle the cranberry-pistachio mixture over the salmon, patting to adhere.

DO AHEAD: The vinaigrette and crusted salmon can be made 1 day ahead. Store the vinaigrette in a container and refrigerate. Cover the salmon with plastic wrap and refrigerate.

Bake the salmon uncovered until it is just cooked through, about 18 minutes. Using the foil as an aid, carefully lift the salmon from the baking sheet and allow the salmon to slide from the foil onto a long oval or rectangular platter.

Serve the salmon warm at room temperature, or cold with the vinaigrette.

CHICKEN STRIPS *with* GINGER-APRICOT SAUCE

This dish is a particular favorite of customers with young children, because kids and parents like it equally—and it works great for a picnic, too. Be sure to plan ahead, because the secret of the recipe is that the chicken marinates in the buttermilk mixture for at least 4 hours. If you don't have chicken tenders, simply cut boneless, skinless chicken breasts lengthwise into 1-inch-wide strips.

~ SERVES 6 TO 8 ~

1½	cups buttermilk
3	tablespoons minced shallots
1	teaspoon dried hot red pepper flakes
1	teaspoon minced garlic
1½	teaspoons salt, divided
1	teaspoon freshly ground black pepper, divided
24	chicken tenders (about 2½ pounds total)
4	cups corn oil
2	cups unbleached all-purpose flour
2	teaspoons freshly grated nutmeg
1	teaspoon cayenne pepper
	Ginger-Apricot Sauce, warm (see following recipe)

Whisk the buttermilk, shallots, red pepper flakes, garlic, ½ teaspoon of the salt, and ½ teaspoon of the black pepper in a large bowl to blend. Add the chicken tenders. Cover and refrigerate for at least 4 hours or up to 24 hours.

Preheat the oven to 400°F. Heat the oil in a heavy large frying pan over medium-high heat until a deep-fry thermometer registers 400°F. Meanwhile, mix the flour, nutmeg, cayenne pepper, remaining 1 teaspoon of salt, and remaining ½ teaspoon of black pepper in another large bowl.

Remove 6 chicken tenders from the buttermilk mixture, then dip them, one at a time, in to the flour mixture and turn to coat completely. Fry the coated chicken tenders until crisp and pale golden, about 2 minutes on each side. Remove the chicken tenders and place them on a baking rack set on a rimmed baking sheet; set aside to allow the excess oil to drip away from the chicken. Repeat coating and frying the remaining chicken tenders in 3 more batches. When all the chicken tenders are fried, bake them until they are no longer pink in the middle, about 10 minutes.

Serve warm with the sauce.

GINGER-APRICOT SAUCE

This sauce is terrific with lots of foods. We love it with dim sum! Note that all the alcohol burns off in the cooking, so the sauce is fine for children and nondrinkers.

MAKES 4¾ CUPS

- 2 cups apricot nectar
- 1½ cups dry white wine
- 1 cup dried apricots, quartered
- ½ cup sugar
- ½ cup water
- ¼ cup minced peeled fresh ginger
- 2 tablespoons Asian chili garlic sauce

Combine all the ingredients in a heavy large saucepan. Bring the mixture to a boil over medium-high heat. Reduce the heat to low, cover the saucepan, and simmer until the apricots are very tender and the liquids reduce slightly, about 30 minutes. Cool slightly.

Working in batches, puree the sauce in a blender until smooth.

DO AHEAD: The sauce can be made 3 days ahead. Cool, then cover and refrigerate. Rewarm in a heavy medium saucepan over medium heat, stirring occasionally, until hot.

TOMATO, BASIL PESTO *and* THREE-CHEESE STRATA

The egg/bread/milk/cheese baked dish called the strata is a classic every cook should know how to make. It works beautifully on a buffet table, it needs to be assembled the night before and popped into the oven just before brunch (or dinner), and you can customize it however you like. I love this particular strata, as do our customers, but you can experiment with different herbs, cheese mixtures, and cut-up cooked Italian sausages, bacon, or ham.

~ SERVES 8 TO 10 ~

3	cups heavy cream
2	cups whole milk
6	extra-large eggs
1	teaspoon salt, plus more for seasoning
¾	teaspoon freshly ground black pepper, plus more for seasoning
2½	cups (about 8 ounces) shredded sharp Cheddar cheese
1½	cups (about 6 ounces) shredded mozzarella cheese
½	cup (about 2 ounces) freshly grated Parmesan cheese
1	1½-pound loaf French or sourdough bread, cut into ½-inch-thick slices
8	plum tomatoes (about 1½ pounds total), sliced crosswise
1	cup chopped fresh basil
6	tablespoons Basil-Parsley Pesto (page 32)

Preheat the oven to 350°F. Butter a 13 x 9 x 2-inch baking dish. Whisk the cream, milk, eggs, 1 teaspoon of salt, and ¾ teaspoon of pepper in a large bowl to blend. Toss the Cheddar cheese, mozzarella cheese, and Parmesan cheese in another bowl to blend.

Layer a third of the bread slices over the bottom of the buttered baking dish and top with a third of the tomato slices. Sprinkle the tomatoes with salt and pepper, then half of the chopped basil, and a third of the cheese mixture (about 1½ cups). Pour a third (about 1¾ cups) of the custard over. Top with a second layer of bread, and spread all of the pesto over the bread. Arrange half of the remaining tomato slices over the bread and sprinkle with salt and pepper. Top with half of the remaining chopped basil and half of the remaining cheese mixture. Pour half of the remaining custard over. Repeat with a third layering of the remaining bread, tomatoes, salt and pepper, chopped basil, and custard. Sprinkle the remaining cheese mixture over. Bake uncovered until puffed and golden on top and a knife comes out clean when inserted into the center of the strata, about 50 minutes.

CHICKEN and MUSHROOM BREAD PUDDING with TARRAGON and GRUYÈRE CHEESE

Bread puddings aren't just for dessert—this recipe has all the custardy richness of a sweet bread pudding, but it's a savory main course instead. At the restaurant we make this with our house-made rosemary-currant bread, but any rosemary bread or French bread works well.

~ SERVES 8 TO 10 ~

¼	cup (½ stick) unsalted butter
1	cup sliced leeks (white and pale green parts only)
2	cups (about 4 ounces) sliced stemmed fresh shiitake mushrooms
2	cups (about 12 ounces) diced cooked boneless skinless chicken breast
2	tablespoons chopped fresh tarragon
2	teaspoons salt
1	teaspoon freshly ground black pepper
8	ounces French bread, cubed (about 6 cups)
2	cups chicken stock
4	cups heavy cream
10	extra-large eggs
1½	cups shredded Gruyère cheese, divided
1	tablespoon Tabasco sauce

Preheat the oven to 350°F. Butter a 13 x 9 x 2-inch baking dish. Melt the butter in a heavy large sauté pan over medium heat. Add the leeks and sauté until they soften, about 2 minutes. Add the mushrooms and sauté until they are tender, about 8 minutes. Add the chicken, tarragon, salt, and pepper. Cook for several more minutes to allow the flavors to blend. Stir in the bread cubes, then the chicken stock.

Whisk the cream and eggs in a large bowl to blend, then stir in 1 cup of the Gruyère cheese and the Tabasco. Fold in the chicken mixture. Transfer the mixture to the prepared baking dish.

DO-AHEAD: The bread pudding can be made up to this point 1 day ahead. Cover and refrigerate.

Sprinkle the remaining ½ cup of Gruyère cheese over the bread pudding and bake uncovered until the bread pudding puffs and is golden brown on top, about 1 hour and 10 minutes.

BABY BACK PORK RIBS *with* ESPRESSO BARBECUE GLAZE

A summertime classic, these ribs are first baked, to set the glaze, and then finished either on the grill or in the oven. Don't worry if you don't have an espresso machine—simply pick up some espresso at your local coffee shop or dissolve espresso powder in hot water.

~ SERVES 6 ~

RIBS:

 3 racks baby back ribs (about 6 pounds total)
 2 tablespoons olive oil
 1 teaspoon salt
 1 teaspoon freshly ground black pepper

BARBECUE GLAZE:

 1 cup freshly brewed espresso
 1 cup ketchup
 ½ cup balsamic vinegar
 ½ cup soy sauce
 ¼ cup clover honey
 2 tablespoons minced garlic
 1 tablespoon chili powder
 1 teaspoon freshly ground black pepper
 1 teaspoon salt

TO PREPARE THE RIBS: Preheat the oven to 350°F. Brush the ribs with the olive oil, and sprinkle with salt and pepper. Place the ribs on a heavy large rimmed baking sheet and cover tightly with foil. Bake until the meat between the ribs is tender, about 2 hours.

MEANWHILE, TO PREPARE THE BARBECUE GLAZE: Combine all the ingredients in a heavy large saucepan and bring to a simmer over medium-high heat. Reduce the heat to medium-low and simmer until the mixture thickens slightly, about 15 minutes.

DO AHEAD: The baked ribs and barbecue glaze can be made 1 day ahead. Cool completely, then pour off any excess liquid from the ribs and cover the ribs on the baking sheet. Store the glaze in a container. Keep the ribs and glaze refrigerated.

Increase the oven temperature to 450°F. Brush some of the glaze over the ribs. Bake uncovered, bone side up, for 10 minutes. Turn the ribs over and baste the meaty side again with more glaze. Continue baking for 10 minutes. Cut the racks between the bones into individual ribs. Alternately, these ribs can be grilled. To do so, preheat a barbecue for medium heat. Brush the ribs with the glaze and grill them for 10 minutes. Turn them over and brush the ribs with more glaze. Continue grilling until the ribs are heated through, about 10 minutes longer, brushing the ribs with additional glaze as they cook.

Rewarm the remaining glaze in a small saucepan over medium-low heat and serve it in a bowl alongside the ribs, if desired.

CHICKEN BREASTS *with* CHERRY-RHUBARB CHUTNEY

A quick, easy, and downright delicious weeknight supper entrée, this recipe is made even simpler if you prepare the chutney a day or two in advance. Steam some rice and roast some asparagus, and you've got a lovely spring dinner.

~ SERVES 6 ~

CHERRY-RHUBARB CHUTNEY:

- 1 cup sugar
- 1/3 cup apple cider vinegar
- 2 tablespoons minced peeled fresh ginger
- 1 tablespoon minced garlic
- 1 teaspoon ground cinnamon
- 1 teaspoon ground cumin
- 1/4 teaspoon ground allspice
- 1 pound fresh rhubarb, halved lengthwise, then cut crosswise
- 1 cup diced red onion
- 1 cup dried tart cherries

CHICKEN:

- 1 tablespoon ground cumin
- 1/2 teaspoon kosher salt
- 1/4 teaspoon coarsely ground black pepper
- 6 boneless chicken breasts with skin
- 1 tablespoon (or more) olive oil

TO PREPARE THE CHERRY-RHUBARB CHUTNEY: Combine the sugar, vinegar, ginger, garlic, cinnamon, cumin, and allspice in a large saucepan. Bring to a simmer over low heat, stirring until the sugar dissolves. Stir in the rhubarb, red onions, and cherries. Increase the heat to medium-high and cook until the rhubarb is tender and begins to fall apart, stirring often, about 5 minutes.

DO-AHEAD: The chutney can be made up to this point 3 days ahead. Cool, cover, and refrigerate.

TO PREPARE THE CHICKEN: Preheat the oven to 400°F. Mix the cumin, salt, and pepper in a small bowl to blend. Rub the spice mixture over the chicken breasts. Heat 1 tablespoon of oil in a heavy large sauté pan over medium-high heat. Place 3 chicken breasts, skin side down, in the pan and cook until the skin is crisp and golden brown, about 4 minutes. Set the chicken, skin side up, on a rimmed baking sheet. Repeat with the remaining 3 chicken breasts, adding more oil to the pan if needed.

Spoon some chutney over each chicken breast and bake until the chicken is just cooked through, about 15 minutes. Transfer the chicken to plates and spoon some of the remaining chutney over the chicken and serve.

BLACKBERRY POLENTA BREAD PUDDING

The polenta bread is more like a rich pound cake with cornmeal than an actual cornbread, and it's wonderfully delicious on its own—sauces not required. Folding the whipped egg whites into the bread batter helps it rise and gives it a light, fluffy texture. Feel free to substitute other berries for the blackberries.

~ **SERVES 8 TO 10** ~

POLENTA BREAD:

	Nonstick cooking spray
¾	cup unbleached all-purpose flour
⅔	cup yellow cornmeal
1	tablespoon baking powder
½	teaspoon salt
1	cup (2 sticks) unsalted butter, at room temperature
1	cup sugar
4	extra-large eggs, separated
2	extra-large egg yolks

CUSTARD:

6	cups heavy cream
1½	vanilla beans, split lengthwise
15	extra-large egg yolks
1½	cups sugar
1½	6-ounce containers fresh blackberries
	Sweetened whipped cream (optional)

TO MAKE THE POLENTA BREAD: Preheat the oven to 350°F. Spray a 9 x 5 x 3-inch loaf pan with nonstick spray. Whisk the flour, cornmeal, baking powder, and salt in a medium bowl to blend. Using an electric mixer with the paddle attachment, beat the butter and sugar in a large bowl until light and fluffy. Beat in the 6 egg yolks, adding 1 at a time and blending well after each addition. Add the cornmeal mixture and mix just until blended.

Using an electric mixer with the whisk attachment, beat the 4 egg whites in a clean large bowl until stiff peaks form when the whisk is lifted. Stir one-third of the egg whites into the batter to lighten it, then fold in the remaining egg whites (the batter will be thick). Immediately spread the batter in the prepared pan and bake until a tester inserted into the center of the bread comes out clean and the top is dark golden brown, about 50 minutes. Maintain the oven temperature.

Cut the bread into 1-inch cubes or cut it crosswise into ½-inch-thick slices. Arrange the bread in a single layer on a heavy large baking sheet and bake until the bread is lightly browned, about 15 minutes. Set aside to cool completely.

MEANWHILE, TO MAKE THE CUSTARD: Place the cream in a heavy large saucepan. Scrape the seeds from the vanilla beans into the cream and add the beans. Bring just to a simmer over medium-high heat, then remove from the heat. Whisk the egg yolks and sugar in a large bowl to blend. Gradually whisk the hot cream into the yolk mixture. Strain the mixture into another large bowl and let cool.

DO AHEAD: The bread and custard can be made up to this point 2 days ahead. Cover the bread and store at room temperature. Keep the custard refrigerated.

TO ASSEMBLE AND BAKE THE BREAD PUDDING: Butter a 13 x 9 x 2-inch baking dish. Arrange the toasted bread in the prepared baking dish. If using slices, overlap them slightly in the dish. Toss the berries in the custard to coat. Pour the custard over the bread, distributing the berries evenly. Set aside for 30 minutes to allow the bread to soften and absorb some of the custard. Bake until the custard simmers gently in the center, about 35 minutes.

Spoon the warm pudding onto plates and serve with the sweetened whipped cream if desired.

LEMON SOUFFLÉ PUDDING CAKE

I grew up with a backyard full of what seemed to me to be every type of fruit tree, but most of all we had lemons. So my mother made this cake every week, and it never failed to delight my sisters and me. As it bakes, it forms a custard on the bottom and a soft spongy layer on top; I like to spoon the cake and custard into glass dessert bowls and garnish with fresh blackberries, blueberries, and/or raspberries, along with lemon-basil sprigs. You can serve this warm, at room temperature, or cold.

~ **SERVES 8 TO 10** ~

1½	cups granulated sugar
½	cup (1 stick) unsalted butter, at room temperature
6	extra-large eggs, separated
⅔	cup fresh lemon juice
1	tablespoon finely grated lemon zest (from 2 large lemons)
⅔	cup unbleached all-purpose flour
2	cups whole milk
1	cup heavy cream
½	teaspoon salt
	Powdered sugar, for garnish
	Assorted fresh berries (such as blackberries, blueberries, and raspberries), for garnish

Position the oven rack in the center of the oven and preheat the oven to 350°F. Using an electric mixer with the paddle attachment, beat the granulated sugar and butter in a large bowl until the mixture is light and fluffy. Add the 6 egg yolks 1 at a time, beating well after each addition. Beat in the lemon juice and lemon zest, then mix in the flour. Add the milk and cream and stir until the mixture is well blended.

Using an electric mixer with the whisk attachment, beat the egg whites and salt in a clean large bowl until soft peaks form when the whisk is lifted. Stir one-fourth of the egg whites into the lemon mixture, then gently fold in the remaining whites.

Pour the batter into a 13 x 9 x 2-inch baking dish. Set the baking dish in a roasting pan. Set the roasting pan in the center rack in the oven and pour enough hot water into the roasting pan to come halfway up the sides of the baking dish. Bake until the cake is just set and golden on top, about 50 minutes. Let cool slightly.

Remove the baking dish from the water bath. Spoon the warm pudding cake into dessert bowls. Dust with powdered sugar, scatter the berries over, and serve.

HUMMINGBIRD CAKE
with BANANA, PINEAPPLE and PECANS

I love this timeless Southern layer cake for its wonderful sweetness—some say that's why it's called a Hummingbird cake, because hummingbirds love ultra-sweet nectar. Regardless of the name, it's a real crowd-pleaser, and it's good for a crowd, too, because it serves up to 16. It is a popular cake in springtime, especially for Easter.

~ SERVES 12 TO 16 ~

CAKE:

	Nonstick cooking spray
3	cups cake flour, plus more for dusting
1	teaspoon baking soda
1	teaspoon ground cinnamon
1	teaspoon salt
2	cups sugar
1½	cups canola oil
3	extra-large eggs
½	teaspoon vanilla extract
½	teaspoon almond extract
6	ripe bananas, coarsely mashed (about 2 cups)
1	cup drained crushed pineapple
1	cup flaked sweetened coconut
1	cup pecans, chopped

FROSTING:

2	8-ounce packages cream cheese, at room temperature
1	cup (2 sticks) unsalted butter, at room temperature
2	pounds powdered sugar, sifted
2	teaspoons vanilla extract
	Toasted shaved coconut, for garnish

TO PREPARE THE CAKE: Position the oven rack in the center of the oven and preheat the oven to 350°F. Spray three 9-inch-diameter cake pans with nonstick spray. Line the pans with parchment paper. Spray the paper with nonstick spray and dust with flour to coat the paper and sides of the pan; tap out the excess flour.

Whisk the flour, baking soda, cinnamon, and salt in a large bowl to blend. Using an electric mixer with the paddle attachment, beat the sugar, oil, eggs, vanilla, and almond extract in a large bowl until well blended. Stir in the flour mixture. Fold in the bananas, pineapple, coconut, and pecans.

Divide the batter evenly among the prepared pans. Bake until a toothpick inserted into the center of the cakes comes out clean, about 25 minutes. Transfer the pans to a cooling rack and cool for 10 minutes. Invert the cakes onto the cooling rack and cool completely.

TO FROST THE CAKE: Using an electric mixer with a clean paddle attachment, beat the cream cheese and butter in a large bowl until light and fluffy. With the mixer on low speed, gradually beat in the powdered sugar. Once all the powdered sugar has been added, continue to beat until the frosting is fluffy. Beat in the vanilla extract.

Arrange 1 cake layer on a platter flat side up. Spread 1¼ cups of frosting over the top of the cake. Top with the second cake layer, flat side down. Spread 1¼ cups of frosting over the top. Top with the third cake layer, flat side up. Spread half of the remaining frosting all over the cake. Refrigerate until the frosting is set, about 1 hour. Spread the remaining frosting all over the cake. Press the toasted coconut around the sides of the cake. Cut the cake into wedges and serve.

DO AHEAD: The cake can be prepared 1 day ahead. Cover the cake with a cake dome and refrigerate. Let stand at room temperature 1 hour before serving.

APPLE PIE CAKE *with* WHISKEY CARAMEL SAUCE

This favorite family recipe is a homey cake that can be whipped together for an easy weeknight family dessert. The apples aren't peeled, which makes it that much easier to put together. Don't be alarmed by the high proportion of apples to batter—it comes out beautifully. This cake is best served warm, but it's also good at room temperature.

~ SERVES 8 ~

	Nonstick cooking spray
1	cup unbleached all-purpose flour
1	teaspoon ground cinnamon
1	teaspoon salt
½	teaspoon baking soda
1	cup sugar
¼	cup (½ stick) unsalted butter, at room temperature
1	extra-large egg
2	tablespoons hot water
1	teaspoon vanilla extract
1½	large tart green apples (such as Granny Smith), cored, cut into ½-inch pieces (about 3 cups)
½	cup coarsely chopped walnuts
	Whiskey Caramel Sauce, warmed (page 87)

Preheat the oven to 350°F. Spray an 8-inch-diameter springform pan with nonstick cooking spray. Sift the flour, cinnamon, salt, and baking soda into a medium bowl. Using an electric mixer with the paddle attachment, beat the sugar and butter in a large bowl until light in color and fluffy. Add the egg and beat to blend well. Beat in the hot water and vanilla to blend well. Add the flour mixture and beat on low speed just until blended. Using a large silicone spatula, fold the apples and nuts into the batter.

Transfer the batter to the prepared pan, spreading evenly. Bake until the apples are tender, the top is dark golden brown, and the cake pulls away from the sides of the pan, about 40 minutes.

Run a knife around the pan sides to loosen the cake from the pan. Remove the pan sides and transfer the cake to a platter. Cut the warm cake into wedges and transfer to plates. Spoon the caramel sauce over and serve.

WHISKEY CARAMEL SAUCE

MAKES 2¼ CUPS

1½	cups sugar
⅓	cup water
1½	cups heavy cream
2½	tablespoons whiskey

Stir the sugar and the water in a heavy medium saucepan over medium-low heat until the sugar dissolves. Increase the heat and boil without stirring until the syrup turns a deep amber color, brushing down the sides of the pan with a moistened pastry brush and swirling the pan occasionally, about 8 minutes. Whisk in the cream (the mixture will bubble vigorously). Stir until the sauce thickens slightly, about 2 minutes. Whisk in the whiskey.

DO AHEAD: The sauce can be prepared 2 days ahead. Cover and refrigerate. Rewarm over medium heat before serving.

SPICED PUMPKIN CHEESECAKE *with* GINGERSNAP CRUST

The key to giving this cheesecake the perfect creamy texture is baking it in a water bath. And the key to ensuring that the water doesn't leak into the crust and make it soggy is wrapping the springform pan with a triple layer of heavy-duty foil, making sure the sides of the foil are higher than the water bath. No matter how new or tight-fitting the springform pan is, water will leak through if the pan is not wrapped with a sturdy foil.

~ SERVES 12 ~

CRUST:

       Nonstick cooking spray

13   ounces gingersnap cookies

¾   cup walnuts

¼   cup sugar

5   tablespoons unsalted butter, melted

FILLING:

3   8-ounce packages cream cheese, at room temperature

1⅓   cups sugar

1   teaspoon ground cinnamon

½   teaspoon ground ginger

¼   teaspoon freshly grated nutmeg

¼   teaspoon ground allspice

¼   teaspoon ground cloves

½   teaspoon salt

1   15-ounce can pumpkin puree

1   tablespoon fresh lemon juice

1   tablespoon vanilla extract

5   extra-large eggs, at room temperature

1   cup heavy cream

       Whiskey Caramel Sauce, warmed (see following recipe)

TO PREPARE THE CRUST: Position the oven rack in the center of the oven and preheat the oven to 350°F. Spray a 9-inch springform pan with 2¾-inch-high sides with non-stick cooking spray. Grind the gingersnap cookies in a food processor until very fine crumbs form (you will have about 2½ cups of cookie crumbs). Add the walnuts and sugar and blend until the nuts are finely ground. Transfer the mixture to a medium bowl and stir in the butter. Press the mixture evenly over the bottom and all the way up the sides of the prepared pan. Bake until lightly browned, about 15 minutes.

Cool completely. Wrap the outside of the pan in a triple layer of wide heavy-duty foil.

TO PREPARE THE FILLING: Using an electric mixer with the paddle attachment, beat the cream cheese in a large bowl until soft and no lumps remain, scraping down the sides of the bowl and the beater occasionally, about 2 minutes. Add the sugar, spices, and salt and beat until well blended, scraping the sides and bottom of the bowl and the beater occasionally. It is important that the cream cheese and

TO PREPARE THE FILLING: Using an electric mixer with the paddle attachment, beat the cream cheese in a large bowl until soft and no lumps remain, scraping down the sides of the bowl and the beater occasionally, about 2 minutes. Add the sugar, spices, and salt and beat until well blended, scraping the sides and bottom of the bowl and the beater occasionally. It is important that the cream cheese and sugar are very well blended and no lumps of cheese remain, or else bits of the cheese will be visible in the cheesecake. Mix in the pumpkin, lemon juice, and vanilla. Mix in 3 eggs until well blended, then beat in the remaining 2 eggs. Add the cream and beat on low speed just until blended. Scrape the bowl and give the batter a final stir by hand.

Pour the batter into the crust, filling the crust completely. You will have about ¾ cup of batter left over; you can discard the extra batter or pour it into a custard cup and bake it alongside the cheesecake, if desired. Place the springform pan in a roasting pan. Set the roasting pan on the rack in the oven, then add enough hot water to the roasting pan to come halfway up the sides of the springform pan.

Bake until the edges of the cheesecake are set but the center remains slightly wobbly when the cheesecake is gently shaken, about 1½ hours (the filling will set once it is cold). Cool the cheesecake in the water bath until the water is just warm to the touch. Remove the cheesecake from the water and set it on a wire rack to cool completely. Remove the foil from around the pan sides. Cover and refrigerate the cheesecake in the pan until cold.

DO AHEAD: The cheesecake can be made up to 2 days ahead. Keep it refrigerated.

Remove the pan sides from the cheesecake and cut the cheesecake into wedges. Transfer to plates, spoon the caramel sauce over, and serve.

SUGAR-CRUSTED NECTARINE, BLUEBERRY *and* TOASTED ALMOND CROUSTADES

I fell in love with croustades the first time I saw them, on a trip to Paris in 1985. They are traditionally open-face, free-form tarts shaped and cooked directly on a baking sheet, but this method just didn't work for us. Our crusts are so tender and buttery they'd collapse and lose their shape during baking. So we use aluminum pie pans (available in the baking aisle of most supermarkets), then unmold them before serving. You can also use individual 4-inch-diameter springform pans.

Make these croustades using whatever fruit is at its peak: pears, quince, or apples during the fall, and apricots, peaches, or plums during the summer. They're delicious served with vanilla ice cream or whipped cream with crystallized ginger.

~ MAKES 8 ~

CRUST:

3	cups unbleached all-purpose flour
1	tablespoon sugar
1½	teaspoons salt
1½	cups (3 sticks) cold unsalted butter, diced
½	cup (about) ice water

FILLING:

⅔	cup granulated sugar
1½	tablespoons unbleached all-purpose flour
2	teaspoons ground cinnamon

2	pounds fresh ripe nectarines, pitted, cut into ½- to ¾-inch cubes
¾	cup fresh blueberries
2	tablespoons (¼ stick) cold unsalted butter, finely diced
1	large egg, beaten with 1 tablespoon water
½	cup sliced blanched almonds
2	tablespoons coarse sugar

TO PREPARE THE CRUST: Mix the flour, sugar, and salt in a food processor. Add the butter and pulse just until the mixture resembles a coarse meal. Drizzle ½ cup of the ice water over the dough and pulse just until the dough pulls away from the sides of the bowl (the mixture will still look crumbly). Add more ice water by teaspoonfuls to moisten, if necessary. Transfer the dough to a work surface and press the dough into a ball. Divide the dough into 8 equal pieces. Flatten each piece into a disc and wrap each disc in plastic. Refrigerate at least 1 hour and up to 2 days.

TO PREPARE THE FILLING AND ASSEMBLE THE CROUSTADES: Preheat the oven to 375°F. Stir the granulated sugar, flour, and cinnamon in a large bowl to blend. Add the nectarines and blueberries and toss to coat. Set aside while rolling out the crusts, tossing the fruit occasionally.

Roll out each dough disc on a lightly floured work surface to a 7-inch-diameter round. Line eight 4-inch-diameter aluminum pie pans or 4-inch-diameter springform pans with the dough discs. Divide the fruit filling among the dough-lined pans. Dot the fruit filling with the butter. Fold the dough edges over a portion of the filling, softly pleating the edges. Cover and refrigerate until the dough is cold and firm, about 30 minutes.

DO AHEAD: The croustades can be made up to this point 1 day ahead. Keep refrigerated.

Brush the crusts with the beaten egg mixture. Sprinkle the almonds, then the coarse sugar over the croustades. Bake until the pastry is golden brown and the filling bubbles, about 55 minutes. Cool slightly. Using a small flexible silicone spatula, loosen the crusts from the pans, then remove the croustades. Serve the croustades warm or at room temperature.

LEMON COCONUT BARS

Who would have guessed that a simple recipe from a 1930s spiral-bound ladies guild cookbook from Minnesota would be made every single day in our kitchens? My mother made these lemon bars for us every week, painstakingly juicing the lemons from our trees. I think it's the shortbread crust and the layering of the creamy lemon filling and coconut topping that make it so special.

~ MAKES 12 TO 16 SQUARES ~

CRUST:

Nonstick cooking spray
2   cups unbleached all-purpose flour
½   cup powdered sugar
1   cup (2 sticks) cold unsalted butter, cut into cubes

FILLING:

2¾   cups granulated sugar
6   extra-large eggs
1   cup fresh lemon juice
Zest of 3 large lemons (about 1½ tablespoons)
⅔   cup unbleached all-purpose flour
1½   teaspoons baking powder
1½   cups flaked sweetened coconut
Powdered sugar, for garnish

TO PREPARE THE CRUST: Preheat the oven to 350°F. Spray a 12 x 9 x 1-inch baking pan with nonstick spray. Mix the flour and powdered sugar in a food processor to blend. Add the butter and pulse until the mixture resembles a coarse meal. Sprinkle the mixture over the prepared baking pan and press the dough evenly over the bottom of the pan. Bake until the crust is golden, about 20 minutes. Transfer the pan to a rack and cool completely. Maintain the oven temperature.

TO PREPARE THE FILLING: Whisk the granulated sugar and eggs in a large bowl to blend. Whisk in the lemon juice and lemon zest. Whisk in the flour and baking powder. Mix in the coconut. Transfer the mixture to the cooled crust. Bake until the top is golden brown and the filling is just set in the center when the pan is gently shaken, about 40 minutes. Transfer the pan to a rack and cool completely. Dust the top with powdered sugar. Cut into squares. Transfer the lemon bars to a platter and serve.

DO AHEAD: The lemon bars can be made 1 day ahead. Wrap with plastic and refrigerate. Let come to room temperature before serving.

GRAHAM CRACKER CHEWY BARS

I adapted this recipe from one of my favorite books, Nantucket Open-House Cookbook, *by Sarah Leah Chase. I love watching people's expressions when they bite into these bars for the first time. The textures and flavors—rich toffee, a chewy center, and a crunchy bottom—make everyone smile. The secret is not to overbake the crust. Serve them at room temperature, so the flavors meld together.*

~ MAKES 24 BARS ~

CRUST:

3	cups graham cracker crumbs
¾	cup (1½ sticks) unsalted butter, at room temperature
¼	cup sugar
2	tablespoons unbleached all-purpose flour

TOPPING:

2½	cups (packed) golden brown sugar
4	extra-large eggs
⅔	cup graham cracker crumbs
1	tablespoon vanilla extract
¾	teaspoon salt
½	teaspoon baking powder
1	cup pecans, chopped

TO PREPARE THE CRUST: Preheat the oven to 350°F. Using an electric mixer, beat the graham cracker crumbs, butter, sugar, and flour in a large bowl until moist and well blended. Press the mixture firmly and evenly over the bottom of a 13 x 9 x 2-inch baking pan. Bake until the crust is golden brown, about 10 minutes.

MEANWHILE, TO PREPARE THE TOPPING: Whisk the brown sugar and eggs in a large bowl to blend. Add the graham cracker crumbs, vanilla, salt, and baking powder and stir until well blended. Stir in the pecans. Spread the mixture over the baked crust and bake until the filling is dark golden on top and moves slightly when the pan is gently shaken, about 25 minutes. Transfer the pan to a cooling rack and cool completely. Cut into 24 squares. Transfer the bars to a platter to serve.

DO AHEAD: The bars can be made 1 day ahead. Wrap with plastic and keep at room temperature.

CRYSTALLIZED GINGER COOKIES

These are soft and slightly chewy cookies with a spicy ginger flavor. They are always a good complement to ice cream, they're lovely with tea, and they hit the spot whenever you want something a little sweet … but not too much.

~ MAKES 12 COOKIES ~

2	cups unbleached all-purpose flour
1	teaspoon ground ginger
¾	teaspoon baking powder
½	teaspoon salt
1	cup (2 sticks) unsalted butter, at room temperature
1	cup (packed) golden brown sugar
1	extra-large egg yolk
½	cup finely chopped crystallized ginger

Preheat the oven to 325°F. Line 2 heavy large baking sheets with parchment paper. Sift the flour, ground ginger, baking powder, and salt into a medium bowl. Using an electric mixer with the paddle attachment, beat the butter and sugar in a large bowl until lighter in color and fluffy. Add the egg yolk and beat until well blended. Mix in the crystallized ginger. Add the flour mixture and mix on low speed just until blended.

Using a scant ¼ cup of dough for each cookie, spoon the dough onto the prepared baking sheets, spacing evenly apart. Using the bottom of a glass, press the cookies into 3-inch-diameter rounds. Bake until the cookies puff and are very pale golden brown, about 10 minutes (do not overbake). Transfer the cookies to a rack and cool slightly. Serve warm or at room temperature.

DO AHEAD: The cookies can be made up to 1 day ahead. Store in an airtight container at room temperature.

CHOCOLATE ESPRESSO CREAM CHEESE BARS

Brownies are pretty much impossible to resist when they come out of the oven—and they get even better when you add a layer of espresso-infused cream cheese and some chocolate ganache. We serve large 3-inch-square bars at the market, but you can cut them any size you like.

~ MAKES 16 TO 20 BARS ~

BROWNIE:

Nonstick cooking spray

1 tablespoon instant espresso powder

1½ teaspoons hot water

4 ounces bittersweet chocolate (56% to 61% cacao), chopped

6 tablespoons (¾ stick) unsalted butter

¾ cup sugar

2 extra-large eggs

1½ teaspoons vanilla extract

½ cup unbleached all-purpose flour

¼ teaspoon salt

½ cup walnuts, chopped

CREAM CHEESE TOPPING:

8 ounces cream cheese, softened

6 tablespoons (¾ stick) unsalted butter, at room temperature

1½ cups powdered sugar

2 teaspoons instant espresso powder

1 teaspoon ground cinnamon

1 teaspoon vanilla extract

1 teaspoon water

CHOCOLATE GLAZE:

1 tablespoon instant espresso powder

2 teaspoons hot water

4 ounces bittersweet chocolate (56% to 61% cacao), finely chopped

⅓ cup heavy cream

1½ tablespoons unsalted butter

TO PREPARE THE BROWNIES: Preheat the oven to 350°F. Spray a 12 x 9 x 1-inch metal baking pan with nonstick cooking spray. Stir the instant espresso and the hot water in a heavy small saucepan until the espresso dissolves. Add the chocolate and butter and stir over medium-low heat until melted and smooth. Set aside to cool slightly.

Using an electric mixer with the paddle attachment, beat

the sugar, eggs, and vanilla in a large bowl to blend well. Mix in the chocolate mixture, then stir in the flour and salt. Fold in the walnuts. Transfer the batter to the prepared pan and bake until a tester inserted into the center comes out with some crumbs attached, about 20 minutes. Transfer the pan to a cooling rack and cool completely.

TO PREPARE THE CREAM CHEESE TOPPING: Using an electric mixer with a clean paddle attachment, beat the cream cheese and butter in a large bowl until light and fluffy. Sift in the powdered sugar. Add the espresso powder, cinnamon, vanilla, and water. Beat until the mixture is well blended. Spread the cream cheese mixture evenly over the cooled brownies and refrigerate until firm, about 30 minutes.

TO PREPARE THE CHOCOLATE GLAZE: Stir the instant espresso and the hot water in a heavy small saucepan to dissolve the espresso. Add the chocolate, cream, and butter and stir over medium-low heat until melted and smooth. Pour the chocolate glaze over the chilled cream cheese topping and spread to cover the top completely. Refrigerate until set, about 3 hours and up to 1 day. Cut into 16 to 20 bars. Transfer the bars to a platter to serve.

DO AHEAD: These bars are best served the day they are baked, but will also be delicious the next day. Cover and keep them refrigerated after the chocolate glaze has set. Cut into bars just before serving.

Although I am no longer a caterer, I spent twenty years of my professional life as one, and many of my happiest memories are of celebrations, from the intimate to the expansive. In fact, so much of what I've learned as a chef comes from my experiences as a caterer. Every good chef must be prepared to deal with challenge—and no one faces challenges like a caterer. You can thoroughly prepare for a party, but the unexpected can always happen. After surviving many surprises, I have learned to be flexible, find a solution, and, above all, concentrate on the guests having a good time—because that's what it's all about.

I have lived through more catering misadventures than I ever thought possible: ovens catching on fire, ingredients forgotten, a fistfight between the rental-company staff and my staff, surprise rainstorms and windstorms, and more. I was once trapped in my station wagon in between courses at a party site while the family's Great Dane, who was not happy about my presence, circled to make sure I stayed in place in my car—while I was needed to serve the dessert course inside. Another time I rented a refrigerated truck to transport the food for a large wedding, and the driver made a sharp turn into an alley, running into a telephone pole. The upper "arm" of the pole speared the top of the truck, trapping it there; fortunately, we had allowed for a four-hour set-up time, and we still got the food ready on time. And then there was the time the marinated tenderloins of pork for a sit-down dinner for fifty were stolen out of our van as we were loading up to head to the party site.

Remarkably, however, we never had a disaster—we were always able to make the best of a mishap. And that is a lesson that every home entertainer must learn. You will encounter surprises and challenges when you throw a celebration, but you will cope with them, and sometimes the party with challenges becomes the most memorable party of all.

Julienne no longer does off-site catering, but we still provide the food for countless celebrations through our Gourmet Market, and over the years we've learned what resonates with people at a party. The biggest dilemma I've faced is how to balance my love for creating new recipes with most people's basic desire to keep eating the dishes they've always loved, especially at Thanksgiving and Christmas. Fortunately, there are excuses to celebrate throughout the year, and some occasions—Mother's Day brunches, birthday dinners, Easter gatherings—allow for plenty of kitchen creativity. And I've been able to combine a respect for tradition with a little creativity in my Thanksgiving and Christmas menus.

In this chapter we detail six celebrations: a Harvest Feast that works beautifully for Thanksgiving, despite its lack of a turkey; an elegant Christmas dinner; a decadent Chocolate Festival for Valentine's Day; a romantic night in Marrakesh for a Moroccan party; a family-friendly Easter meal; and a picnic dinner designed for the Hollywood Bowl, but perfect for any outdoor concert or beach or park picnic. Each celebration takes you from appetizer to dessert—except for the Chocolate Festival, which takes you from dessert to dessert!—and all include dishes you can make ahead. With each, I balance the inventiveness I love with the tradition the occasion demands. So lamb and asparagus, for instance, are at the heart of the Easter meal, but I perk up the lamb with a Mint Salsa Verde, and the asparagus partners with rich Gruyère in a strudel.

My hope is that this chapter will inspire you to bring the people you love together for a celebration built around a great meal. While none of these meals is overly complicated, all do require a certain amount of planning and cooking—and I can assure you, the results are worth it.

Celebrations

—— • ——

Chocolate Festival *103*

A Family Easter *115*

Hollywood Bowl Picnic *125*

An Evening in Morocco *135*

A Harvest Feast *147*

A Winter Celebration *159*

Chocolate Festival

About eight years ago, inspired by seeing the movie *Chocolat*, I decided to have a chocolate festival at Julienne to celebrate Valentine's Day. It's a day of love, and I wanted to show our appreciation to our many and loyal customers. What better way to do it than with chocolate?

We still put on a chocolate festival every Valentine's Day. For this one day a year, it seems entirely appropriate to forget the focus on balanced eating and nutrient-rich vegetables and simply wallow in the romantic joys of sweet chocolate aphrodisiacs.

The seven chocolate-based or chocolate-laced desserts that follow represent many of Julienne's most beloved offerings. Each dessert is pretty, each is rich, and they all will make your guests very happy indeed.

These seven sweets, all of which can be made in advance, would comprise a lovely Saturday-afternoon dessert party during the Valentine season. A chocolate festival for your friends is a great way to celebrate the holiday of love in an inclusive way that's not just focused on couples. Invite your neighbors, invite your single friends, and be sure to invite at least one child— an all-dessert party like this is a child's dream come true.

MENU

Chocolate Crème de Menthe Bars *105*

Chocolate Truffle Brownies *106*

Chocolate Ganache Fondue with Long Stem Strawberries *107*

Coconut Macaroons with Chocolate Raspberry Ganache *109*

Raspberry Jam Hearts *111*

Chocolate Espresso Cookies *112*

Peppermint Shortbread Cookies *113*

CHOCOLATE CRÈME *de* MENTHE BARS

Always a classic combination, dark chocolate and mint form three rich layers: a cakey chocolate bottom, a creamy mint filling, and a dark chocolate ganache finish. These brownie-like bars keep well for several days if refrigerated, and they'll keep even longer in the freezer.

~ MAKES 12 ~

BROWNIES:

  Nonstick cooking spray
3 ounces fine-quality unsweetened chocolate, chopped
6 tablespoons (¾ stick) unsalted butter
¾ cup plus 2 tablespoons unbleached all-purpose flour
3 tablespoons unsweetened Dutch-processed cocoa powder
¾ cup (packed) golden brown sugar
¾ cup granulated sugar
3 extra-large eggs
¼ teaspoon peppermint extract

MINT AND CHOCOLATE TOPPINGS:

2¼ cups powdered sugar, sifted
3 tablespoons plus ¼ cup (½ stick) unsalted butter, at room temperature
1½ tablespoons green-colored crème de menthe
1½ tablespoons half-and-half
4 ounces fine-quality bittersweet chocolate (56% to 60% cacao), chopped

TO PREPARE THE BROWNIES: Position the rack in the center of the oven and preheat the oven to 350°F. Spray a 13 x 9 x 2-inch metal baking pan with nonstick cooking spray. Stir the chocolate and butter in a heavy small saucepan over low heat until melted and smooth, then set aside. Sift the flour and cocoa powder into a medium bowl and set aside.

Using an electric mixer with the paddle attachment, beat the brown sugar, granulated sugar, eggs, and peppermint extract in a large bowl to blend. Add the melted chocolate mixture and beat to blend well. Gradually add the flour mixture, beating just until it is blended and being careful not to overmix the batter. Transfer the batter to the prepared pan.

Bake until a tester inserted into the center comes out with some crumbs attached, about 20 minutes. Transfer the pan to a cooling rack and cool completely.

TO PREPARE THE TOPPINGS: Using an electric mixer with the paddle attachment, slowly mix the powdered sugar and 3 tablespoons of butter in large bowl to blend. Add the crème de menthe and half-and-half. Beat until the mixture is fluffy. Spread a thin layer evenly over the cooled brownies. Refrigerate until the topping is cold.

Stir the chocolate and remaining ¼ cup of butter in a heavy small saucepan over medium-low heat until melted and smooth. Pour the chocolate mixture over the mint filling and spread to coat thinly. Refrigerate until the chocolate topping is firm.

Cut into 12 brownies, forming about 2¼-inch squares.

CHOCOLATE TRUFFLE BROWNIES

These moist, fudgy brownies have the rich and indulgent features of chocolate truffles. If you have a restaurant-quality baking sheet, use it—it makes a difference. This recipe makes enough for a dozen people, so it's great to bring to a party or potluck.

~ MAKES 12 ~

	Nonstick cooking spray
1	pound fine-quality bittersweet chocolate (56% to 60% cacao), chopped
¾	cup (1½ sticks) unsalted butter
1¼	cups sugar
6	extra-large eggs
¼	teaspoon salt
¾	cup cake flour
1½	cups chopped walnuts (about 5 ounces)

Position the oven rack in the center of the oven and preheat the oven to 300°F. Spray a rimmed heavy 12 x 9 x 1-inch baking sheet with nonstick cooking spray, then line the pan with parchment paper. Stir the chocolate and butter in a heavy medium saucepan over medium-low heat until melted and smooth.

Using an electric mixer with the paddle attachment, mix the sugar, eggs, and salt in a large bowl to blend well. Mix in the melted chocolate mixture. Mix in the flour, then the walnuts. Transfer the batter to the prepared pan.

Bake until a tester inserted into the center of the brownies comes out with very moist crumbs attached, about 35 minutes. Transfer the pan to a cooling rack and cool completely. Cut into twenty-four 3-inch-square brownies.

CHOCOLATE GANACHE FONDUE *with* LONG-STEM STRAWBERRIES

Nothing links romance and food together more than dipping strawberries in to warm chocolate. This is a straightforward, classic ganache that everyone loves, but if you're feeling like something more sophisticated, add your favorite liqueur— perhaps framboise or Chambord for a raspberry flavor or Grand Marnier for an orange flavor.

~ SERVES 8 ~

9   ounces fine-quality bittersweet chocolate (56% to 60% cacao), finely chopped
1   cup heavy cream
3   tablespoons unsalted butter, at room temperature
     Fresh long-stem strawberries

Stir the chocolate and cream in a heavy medium saucepan over low heat until melted and smooth, about 5 minutes. Remove the pan from the heat, then add the butter and stir until the butter melts and the mixture is well blended.

Transfer the fondue to a fondue pot and place over a candle flame. Serve with the strawberries for dipping.

COCONUT MACAROONS
with CHOCOLATE RASPBERRY GANACHE

A ganache is a traditional French blend of chocolate and cream. It's liquid enough when warm to pour over cookies, cakes, or fruit; when chilled, it sets up well and can be used in many things, including chocolate truffles. This recipe adds a coulis (puree) of raspberries to delicious effect. Note that the macaroons without the ganache are wonderful to dip into the Chocolate Ganache Fondue (page 107).

~ MAKES 24 ~

MACAROONS:

⅔   cup sweetened condensed milk

1   teaspoon vanilla extract or ½ teaspoon almond extract

⅛   teaspoon salt

3   cups flaked sweetened coconut (about 12 ounces)

2   extra-large egg whites

GANACHE:

1   6-ounce basket fresh raspberries

3   ounces fine-quality bittersweet chocolate (56% to 60% cacao), finely chopped

⅓   cup heavy cream

1   tablespoon unsalted butter, at room temperature

TO PREPARE THE MACAROONS: Position the oven racks in the center and upper third of the oven and preheat the oven to 300°F. Line 2 heavy large baking sheets with parchment paper. Stir the sweetened condensed milk, vanilla extract, and salt in a large bowl to blend well. Stir in the coconut. Using an electric mixer with the whisk attachment, beat the egg whites in another large bowl until stiff peaks form. Fold the beaten egg whites into the coconut mixture. Using about 1½ tablespoons of the coconut mixture for each cookie, spoon the coconut mixture onto the prepared baking sheets, spacing evenly apart. Bake until the edges and tops are lightly brown, about 35 minutes. Transfer to a rack and cool completely.

MEANWHILE, TO PREPARE THE GANACHE: Blend the raspberries in a food processor just until they are pureed.

Strain the puree through a fine-meshed strainer and into a medium bowl. Set the puree aside and discard the seeds.

Stir the chocolate and cream in a heavy small saucepan over medium-low heat until melted and smooth. Remove from the heat, then add the butter and 3 tablespoons of the raspberry puree, whisking until the butter melts and the mixture is well blended. Reserve any remaining raspberry puree for another use.

Dip the macaroons in to the warm ganache. Refrigerate until the ganache is set.

DO AHEAD: The macaroons can be made 2 days ahead. Store in an airtight container and refrigerate.

RASPBERRY JAM HEARTS

This dough is very tender, which makes for a rich and buttery cookie; refrigerating it for an hour makes it easier to roll out. We like the hearts for Valentine's Day, but you can cut the cookies into any shape you like, even simple rounds.

~ MAKES 12 ~

1	cup (2 sticks) unsalted butter, at room temperature
½	cup granulated sugar
2	cups sifted unbleached all-purpose flour
¼	teaspoon salt
1¼	cups ground walnuts
1	cup raspberry preserves
	Powdered sugar, for dusting

Using an electric mixer with the paddle attachment, beat the butter and granulated sugar in a large bowl to blend. Mix in the flour and salt, then the walnuts. Gather the dough into a ball and flatten into 2 discs. Wrap the dough discs with plastic wrap and refrigerate until firm, about 1 hour.

Position the oven racks in the center and upper third of the oven and preheat the oven to 350°F. Line 2 heavy large baking sheets with parchment paper. Roll out 1 dough disc with a floured rolling pin on a floured work surface to about ⅛ inch thickness, lifting the dough and dusting the work surface with flour as you roll out the dough to ensure it does not stick to the surface. Using a 3¼-inch-long heart-shaped cookie cutter, cut out the cookies. Gather the dough scraps and flatten them into a disc, then wrap them in plastic and refrigerate. Transfer the hearts to the prepared baking sheets, spacing 1 inch apart. Using a 1¼-inch heart-shaped cutter, cut a hole in the center of half of the hearts. If desired, bake the small heart-shaped cutouts alongside the cookies.

Bake until the cookies are pale golden around the edges, about 15 minutes. Transfer the cookies to a rack and cool completely. Repeat with the remaining dough disc and reserved chilled dough scraps.

DO AHEAD: The cookies can be made up to this point 1 week ahead. Store in an airtight container and freeze. Thaw the cookies before continuing.

Spread 2 teaspoons of the raspberry preserves over the bottom of 1 whole cookie. Top with a cookie that has a heart-shaped hole, bottom side down, and press gently to adhere. Repeat with the remaining cookies. Dust lightly with powdered sugar.

CHOCOLATE ESPRESSO COOKIES

My sister Vicki made these years ago. We fell in love with them and started selling them at the restaurant. Since then they have been featured in numerous magazines and become a Julienne classic, right up there with our chocolate chunk cookies.

It's best to bake these cookies immediately after the dough is made and allow them to cool completely before removing them from the baking sheet. If you can bake them all at once, do so; if not, bake them in two batches, placing the second batch in the oven as soon as the first batch comes out.

~ MAKES 24 ~

1	pound fine-quality semisweet chocolate, chopped
½	cup (1 stick) unsalted butter
1½	cups sugar
4	extra-large eggs
2	tablespoons instant espresso powder
1	tablespoon vanilla extract
¾	cup unbleached all-purpose flour
½	teaspoon baking powder
½	teaspoon salt
2	cups fine-quality bittersweet chocolate chips (56% to 60% cacao) or ¼-inch chunks
2	cups coarsely chopped walnuts (about 8 ounces)

Position the oven racks in the center and upper third of the oven and preheat the oven to 325°F. Line 4 heavy large baking sheets with parchment paper. Stir the semisweet chocolate and butter in a heavy medium saucepan over medium-low heat until melted and smooth.

Using an electric mixer with the paddle attachment, beat the sugar, eggs, espresso powder, and vanilla in a large bowl for 1 minute, or until blended and slightly foamy. Mix in the melted chocolate mixture. Mix in the flour, baking powder, and salt. Stir in the chocolate chips and walnuts.

Using about 3 tablespoons of the dough for each cookie, spoon the dough onto 2 of the prepared baking sheets, form-ing about 6 cookies per baking sheet. Bake until the cookies are crackled on top and moist in the center, about 14 minutes. Do not overbake so as to keep the center of these cookies moist and fudgy. Transfer the baking sheets to a rack and allow the cookies to cool completely on the baking sheet. The cookies will firm up a bit as they cool, but will still be soft. Repeat baking the remaining cookies. Using a metal spatula, transfer the cookies to a platter and serve.

DO AHEAD: These cookies are best served the day they are baked, but will also be delicious the next day. Store them in an airtight container at room temperature.

PEPPERMINT SHORTBREAD COOKIES

Just a splash of peppermint extract adds zing to these simple chocolate-drizzled shortbread cookies. Instead of peppermint, you can use a couple of teaspoons of lemon, orange, or lime zest.

~ MAKES ABOUT 45 ~

¾	cup (1½ sticks) unsalted butter, at room temperature
½	cup granulated sugar
2	tablespoons (packed) golden brown sugar
1	extra-large egg
1½	teaspoons peppermint extract
½	teaspoon vanilla extract
2	cups unbleached all-purpose flour
⅛	teaspoon salt
2	ounces fine-quality bittersweet chocolate (56% to 60% cacao), chopped

Using an electric mixer with the paddle attachment, beat the butter, granulated sugar, and brown sugar in a large bowl until light and fluffy. Beat in the egg, peppermint extract, and vanilla. Add the flour and salt and mix until a soft dough forms. Divide the dough into 3 equal pieces. Transfer 1 piece of the dough to a sheet of plastic wrap and roll it into a 1½-inch-diameter log that is about 4 inches long. Wrap the log with the plastic to enclose completely. Repeat with the remaining dough, forming 3 logs total. Refrigerate for at least 2 hours or until firm, or freeze for up to 1 week.

Position the oven racks in the center and upper third of the oven and preheat the oven to 350°F. Line 3 heavy large baking sheets with parchment paper. Cut 2 of the logs crosswise into ¼-inch-thick rounds. As you cut out the rounds, the logs will tend to flatten on the bottom, so give the logs a few rolls to maintain their round shape. Arrange the dough rounds on 2 of the prepared baking sheets, spacing evenly apart. Bake until the cookies are light brown around the edges, about 5 minutes. Cool for 5 minutes on the baking sheets, then transfer the cookies to cooling racks to cool completely. Repeat with the remaining dough log.

DO AHEAD: The cookies can be made up to this point 2 weeks ahead. Store in an airtight container and freeze. Thaw before continuing.

Stir the chocolate in a small bowl set over a small saucepan of gently simmering water until the chocolate melts. Drizzle the melted chocolate decoratively over the cooled cookies and set aside until the chocolate is set.

A Family Easter

My daughter Julie hosts our family's Easter potluck every year, and I've always been the Easter Bunny—although because I'm not hopping quite like I used to, last year I bequeathed my bunny costume to my oldest grandchild, Maeve. But everything else stays the same: the colorful clothing, the Easter egg hunt, the table laden with potluck dishes, and the buffet table set under Julie's avocado tree.

The dishes in this section are typical of what we enjoy at our family Easter, and they work well for any celebration of spring. It features the foods most associated with the greening of spring: lamb and baby vegetables, from roasted asparagus and baby carrots to fennel and artichokes. None of these dishes are complicated, all can be prepared in advance, and because they taste good at room temperature, they're perfect for buffets and potlucks.

For my family, the highlight of this meal is dessert: my mother's Rhubarb Meringue Tarts. They combine the most buttery shortbread crust imaginable with creamy rhubarb and a mountain of meringue, and even people who say they don't like rhubarb love these tarts. "We always wanted to eat them first," says Julie. "But they taste even better when held until the end of the meal, and it gives us all a happy occasion to remember Grandma Jolly and keep her spirit alive."

MENU

Leek and Asparagus Strudel *117*

Roasted Leg of Lamb with Gremolata Crust with Mint-Caper Sauce *119*

Roasted Fennel with Baby Carrots, Baby Artichokes and Haricots Verts *121*

Grandma Jolly's Rhubarb Meringue Tarts *123*

LEEK *and* ASPARAGUS STRUDEL

This delicious springtime strudel was inspired by a recipe from the original Silver Palate Cookbook. *It boasts a wonderful savory filling inside and a delicate, flaky pastry. It can be made a day in advance and holds well at room temperature on a buffet table.*

~ MAKES 1 STRUDEL; SERVES 8 ~

- 3 tablespoons plus ½ cup (1 stick) cold unsalted butter, divided
- 2 medium leeks (white and pale green parts only), thinly sliced
- 1 pound asparagus, trimmed, cut diagonally into ½-inch pieces
- 4 ounces Gruyère cheese, grated (about 1 cup)
- 3 extra-large eggs, divided
- 3 tablespoons chopped fresh dill
- 2 tablespoons chopped fresh parsley
- 2 tablespoons fresh lemon juice
- ½ teaspoon salt
- ½ teaspoon freshly ground black pepper
- 9 fresh or frozen phyllo sheets, thawed if frozen (each about 17 x 12 inches)

Melt 3 tablespoons of the cold butter in a heavy large sauté pan over medium heat. Add the leeks and sauté until tender and translucent, about 6 minutes. Add the asparagus and sauté until they are bright green and crisp-tender, about 5 minutes. Remove the pan from the heat and set aside until the asparagus mixture is room temperature. Stir in the cheese, 2 of the eggs, and the dill, parsley, lemon juice, salt, and pepper.

Position the oven rack in the center of the oven and preheat the oven to 350°F. Melt the remaining ½ cup of butter. Brush a heavy large baking sheet lightly with some of the melted butter. Lay 1 phyllo sheet on the work surface and brush lightly with melted butter. Repeat this layering using 7 more phyllo sheets and melted butter. Spoon the asparagus mixture atop the center of the phyllo stack, forming a 12 x 3-inch log and leaving a 2-inch border of phyllo on each short side. Fold the short edges in. Fold 1 inch of the long side furthest from you toward the filling. Beginning at the long side closest to you, roll up the strudel tightly to enclose the filling completely as for a burrito, making sure the ends are tucked in and ending with the 1-inch seam on the bottom. Position the strudel, seam side down, in the center of the prepared baking sheet. Brush some of the remaining melted butter over the sides and ends of the strudel.

Brush the remaining 1 phyllo sheet with the remaining melted butter. Cut the phyllo sheet into 4 squares. Gather each phyllo square together to form 4 loose, free-form rosettes. Beat the remaining 1 egg in a small bowl to blend. Lightly brush the top of the phyllo with the beaten egg (this will act as a glue to help keep the rosettes in place). Set the rosettes atop the strudel.

DO AHEAD: The strudel can be assembled 1 day ahead. Cover and refrigerate.

Bake the strudel uncovered until golden brown, about 55 minutes (a small amount of filling may leak out). Let cool for 20 minutes. Cut the strudel crosswise into slices and serve.

ROASTED LEG OF LAMB
with GREMOLATA CRUST *with* MINT-CAPER SAUCE

We all know that mint and lamb have a natural affinity for each other, but I like to go beyond the standard partnerships, so this sauce is a twist on that tradition. And it doesn't need to be paired only with lamb—try it with grilled steaks or chicken.

This impressive springtime entrée can be made the day before—then on the day of the party, simply pop the lamb in the oven a couple of hours before serving.

~ SERVES 8 ~

SAUCE:

6	tablespoons fresh lemon juice
2	small garlic cloves
2	anchovy fillets
2	tablespoons drained capers, rinsed
¾	cup coarsely chopped fresh parsley
½	cup coarsely chopped fresh mint
2	teaspoons finely chopped fresh oregano
½	cup extra-virgin olive oil
½	teaspoon salt
½	teaspoon freshly ground black pepper

GREMOLATA TOPPING:

1	cup minced fresh parsley
3	tablespoons lemon zest
3	garlic cloves, minced

LAMB:

⅓	cup extra-virgin olive oil
¾	cup finely chopped fresh mint
⅓	cup finely chopped fresh parsley
3	tablespoons minced fresh rosemary
5	garlic cloves, minced
1	5½-pound boneless leg of lamb, well trimmed, butterflied
1	tablespoon kosher salt, plus more for sprinkling
1½	teaspoons freshly ground black pepper, plus more for sprinkling

continued on next page

TO MAKE THE SAUCE: Mix the lemon juice, garlic, anchovies, and capers in a blender until well blended. Add the parsley, mint, and oregano. With the blender running, gradually add the oil, blending until the mixture is smooth. Season to taste with salt and pepper.

TO MAKE THE GREMOLATA: Stir the parsley, lemon zest, and garlic in a medium bowl.

TO PREPARE THE LAMB: Preheat the oven to 450°F. Mix the oil, mint, parsley, rosemary, and garlic in a small bowl. Open the lamb on a work surface. Sprinkle the lamb generously with 1 tablespoon of salt and 1½ teaspoons of pepper and rub into the meat. Spread the herb mixture over the lamb, then roll up the lamb, enclosing the herb mixture completely. Tie the lamb with kitchen string at 2-inch intervals and place the lamb in a roasting pan. Rub any of the excess oil from the bowl over the lamb. Sprinkle the outside of the lamb with more salt and pepper.

DO AHEAD: The sauce, gremolata, and lamb can be prepared up to this point 1 day ahead. Store the sauce and gremolata in separate containers and refrigerate. Wrap the lamb with plastic wrap and refrigerate. Bring the sauce to room temperature and whisk before serving.

Roast the lamb until an instant-read thermometer inserted into the thickest part of the meat registers 120°F, about 1 hour. Sprinkle the gremolata all over the top of the lamb, patting to adhere. Continue roasting until an instant-read thermometer inserted into the thickest part of the meat registers 130°F, tenting the lamb with foil if the gremolata topping begins to brown too quickly, about 30 minutes longer.

Transfer the lamb to a carving board and let rest for 15 minutes. Remove the strings from the lamb. Cut the lamb crosswise into slices and transfer to plates. Serve with the sauce.

ROASTED FENNEL
with BABY CARROTS, BABY ARTICHOKES *and* HARICOT VERTS

Fresh spring vegetables give this side dish color and flavor—look for the best young vegetables you can find. The other key to success with this dish is to divide the vegetables between two baking sheets, so they have enough room to actually roast (instead of steam on a crowded sheet), which gives them a greater depth of flavor. If you're pressed for time, substitute thawed frozen artichoke hearts for fresh—just pat them dry with paper towels before tossing with oil and roast them alongside the other vegetables.

~ SERVES 8 ~

1	lemon
12	baby artichokes
2½	pounds baby carrots, peeled, trimmed
2	medium fennel bulbs, cut into ½-inch-thick wedges
3	tablespoons plus 1 teaspoon olive oil, divided
1	teaspoon kosher salt
½	teaspoon freshly ground black pepper
8	ounces haricot verts, trimmed

Squeeze the juice from the lemon into a large bowl of cold water. Cut the stem off 1 artichoke, leaving about 1 inch. Snap off the bottom 4 rows of leaves or until only the tender yellow-green leaves remain. Cut off the tip of the artichoke. Halve the artichoke lengthwise. Scrape out the choke. Place in the lemon water. Repeat with the remaining 11 artichokes.

Cook the artichokes in a large pot of boiling salted water for 5 minutes. Drain and submerge the artichokes in ice water until cold. Drain again and pat the artichokes dry.

Preheat the oven to 450°F. Toss the artichokes, carrots, and fennel with 3 tablespoons of oil, salt, and pepper in a large bowl. Arrange the vegetable in a single layer on 2 heavy large baking sheets. Roast the vegetables in the oven for 15 minutes. Toss the haricot verts in the same large bowl with the remaining 1 teaspoon of oil, then divide the haricot verts between the baking sheets. Continue roasting the vegetables until they are tender, about 15 minutes longer. Transfer the vegetables to a platter and serve.

GRANDMA JOLLY'S RHUBARB MERINGUE TARTS

Of all the wonderful desserts my mother—who eventually was named Grandma Jolly—was known for, this is my family's favorite. Rich yet delicate crusts are filled with a rosy, sweet-tart rhubarb filling and topped with billowy meringue. They are irresistible.

~ MAKES 8 ~

CRUST:

	Nonstick cooking spray
2½	cups unbleached all-purpose flour
2½	tablespoons sugar
1¼	cups (2½ sticks) cold unsalted butter, cut into pieces

FILLING:

3	cups ½-inch pieces fresh rhubarb (from 3 large stalks)
1½	cups sugar
5	extra-large egg yolks
3	tablespoons unbleached all-purpose flour
¾	teaspoon salt
¾	cup heavy cream

TOPPING:

5	extra-large egg whites
1½	teaspoons vanilla extract
½	cup sugar

FOR THE CRUST: Spray eight 4½-inch-diameter tart pans with removable bottoms with nonstick cooking spray. Blend the flour and sugar in a food processor. Add the butter and blend until a crumbly dough forms. Transfer the dough to a work surface and divide the dough into 8 equal pieces. Form each into a ball and flatten into a disc. Wrap each dough disc in plastic wrap and refrigerate until firm, about 30 minutes.

Preheat the oven to 350°F. Roll out each dough disc on a lightly floured work surface to a 6-inch round. Transfer the dough to the prepared pans, pressing into the pan and trimming the edges.

FOR THE FILLING: Divide the rhubarb among the crusts. Using an electric mixer with the paddle attachment, beat the sugar and egg yolks in a large bowl to blend well. Mix in the flour and salt. Gradually mix in the cream, scraping down the sides of the bowl occasionally. Pour the filling over the rhubarb, dividing equally. Bake until the crusts are pale golden, the rhubarb is tender, and the custard filling is golden brown on top and just set in the center when the pans are gently shaken, about 30 minutes. Transfer the tarts in the pans to a cooling rack and cool completely.

FOR THE MERINGUE TOPPING: Using an electric mixer with the whisk attachment, beat the egg whites in a clean large bowl until foamy. Mix in the vanilla. Gradually add the sugar and beat until stiff, glossy peaks form. Spread the meringue over the tarts. Bake until the meringue is golden brown all over, about 10 minutes. Serve the tarts warm or at room temperature.

Hollywood Bowl Picnic

In 1985, our takeout business was launched when we started making picnics for the Hollywood Bowl. My daughter Jennifer was in high school at the time, and when I had the idea to use Chinese steamer baskets, she and I had a lot of fun assembling them, lining them with kale and filling them with comfort food. We were one of the first L.A. businesses to provide Bowl picnics, and it's still one of our favorite things to prepare for our customers—and for ourselves, when we're fortunate enough to attend a summertime concert.

It's not as easy as you might think to come up with a winning menu for the Hollywood Bowl or any other outdoor event. The food needs to transport well, taste good at room temperature, have a pleasing balance of color, texture, and flavor, and be manageable to eat in often cramped circumstances. The menu I've created here answers all those needs. It also celebrates summer, which

is also what attending an outdoor concert does. Nectarines flavor the salsa with the grilled salmon, the epitome of a summer entrée. Roasted baby courgettes bring to mind July on the Mediterranean. Cracked wheat salad evokes a summer harvest. And nothing says summer like peaches. When my daughters were young, they loved it when I made them whole peach pies, and these are ideal for a picnic, because everyone gets his or her own. And they couldn't be easier to make—you don't even have to pit the peaches.

How you package this picnic will depend on how you'll be sitting at your event. If you're in a box with a table, or on a lawn with a big blanket, you can put containers of food out and let people help themselves. If you're in a tight space, you can portion each meal in advance and give each person his or her own kit. However you do it, this menu will celebrate the summer season in style.

MENU

Wheat Berry Salad with Orange Zest, Pecans and Currants *127*

Salmon with Nectarine–Serrano Chile Salsa *129*

Roasted Baby Courgettes with Olive Oil *130*

Joseph's Limoncello *131*

Whole Peach Dumplings with Honey-Caramel Sauce *133*

WHEAT BERRY SALAD
with ORANGE ZEST, PECANS and CURRANTS

This nutty, subtly sweet grain salad is great for picnics, because it keeps well at room temperature for a good while. You'll find wheat berries at natural foods stores and gourmet markets.

~ SERVES 6 ~

6	cups water
2	cups wheat berries
1½	teaspoons salt, plus more to taste, divided
3	tablespoons freshly squeezed orange juice
2	tablespoons grated orange zest
1½	tablespoons extra-virgin olive oil
½	teaspoon freshly ground black pepper, plus more to taste
1	cup dried currants
1	cup pecans, toasted, coarsely chopped
¼	cup chopped fresh parsley

Combine the water, the wheat berries, and 1 teaspoon of salt in a heavy large saucepan and bring to a boil over high heat. Reduce the heat to medium-low, then cover and simmer, stirring occasionally, until the wheat berries are tender but not mushy, about 1 hour. Transfer the wheat berries to a sieve and drain any excess liquid. Transfer the wheat berries to a large baking sheet and set aside to cool completely.

Stir the orange juice, orange zest, oil, ½ teaspoon of pepper, and remaining ½ teaspoon of salt in a large bowl. Add the wheat berries, currants, pecans, and parsley, and toss thoroughly. Season the salad to taste with more salt and pepper, and serve.

DO AHEAD: The salad can be made up to 1 day ahead. Transfer the salad to a container, then cover and refrigerate. Transport the salad in a cooler to your picnic.

SALMON *with* NECTARINE–SERRANO CHILE SALSA

Nectarines are at their peak in summer, as are the performances at the Hollywood Bowl, so the two make a perfect match. I prefer white nectarines, but yellow will work just fine. And if your picnic is happening outside of nectarine season, not to worry— just serve the salmon with another salsa, such as the Mango-Papaya Salsa (page 39). As for the chiles, serranos are smaller and spicier than jalapeños, but jalapeños make a good substitute. And look for thick salmon filets from the head end, which will cook more evenly.

~ SERVES 6 ~

SALMON:

2 tablespoons (about) olive oil, divided

6 6-ounce skinless salmon filets, each about 1½ inches thick

Salt and freshly ground black pepper

NECTARINE–SERRANO CHILE SALSA:

4 firm but ripe white nectarines (about 1½ pounds total), pitted, cut into ¼-inch pieces

1 serrano chile, seeded, minced

2 tablespoons fresh lime juice

2 tablespoons minced fresh cilantro

1 tablespoon minced fresh mint leaves

Salt and freshly ground black pepper

TO PREPARE THE SALMON: Preheat the oven to 350°F. Lightly coat a heavy rimmed baking sheet with ½ tablespoon of the oil. Sprinkle the salmon with salt and pepper. Heat 1 tablespoon of the oil in a large skillet over high heat. Place 3 salmon filets, top side down, in the skillet and cook just until they are golden on the bottom, about 2 minutes. Transfer the salmon, golden side up, to the prepared baking sheet. Repeat with the remaining 3 salmon filets, and adding more oil to the skillet, if needed. Bake until the salmon is just opaque in the center, about 13 minutes.

MEANWHILE, TO PREPARE THE NECTARINE–SERRANO CHILE SALSA: Toss the first 5 ingredients in a medium bowl. Season to taste with salt and pepper.

DO AHEAD: The salmon and salsa can be made up to 1 day ahead. Refrigerate the salmon until cool, then transfer it to a container in a single layer and keep refrigerated. Enclose the salsa in a separate container and refrigerate. Transport the salmon and salsa in a cooler to your picnic.

Transfer the salmon filets to plates. Spoon the salsa over and serve.

ROASTED BABY COURGETTES *with* OLIVE OIL

With all the other flavors going on in the salmon, salsa, and salad, I like a simple vegetable side dish. These baby courgettes (French for zucchini) are simply roasted with a little olive oil. If you want to jazz them up just a little more, toss them with finely chopped fresh tarragon, dill, basil, or parsley as soon as they're out of the oven.

~ SERVES 6 ~

- 1 pound baby courgettes
- 1 tablespoon extra-virgin oil
- ½ teaspoon kosher salt
- ½ teaspoon freshly ground black pepper

Position the oven rack in the center of the oven and pre-heat the oven to 450°F. Toss the courgettes with the oil on a rimmed heavy baking sheet to coat, then sprinkle with the salt and pepper. Roast until they are crisp-tender and beginning to brown, jostling the courgettes after the first 6 minutes, and roasting them for about 12 minutes total. Store them in a container and transport them in a basket to your picnic.

JOSEPH'S LIMONCELLO

Julie and I invited my food-obsessed art director Joseph Shuldiner to join us for a concert and picnic at our box at the Holly-wood Bowl. After our meal, he brought out an iced bottle of his Limoncello to share as a digestif, and ever since then, we've each received a beautiful bottle as a holiday gift. This zesty, tangy liqueur hails from southern Italy, where citrus thrives. With just four ingredients, it is both simple and inexpensive to make—and homemade Limoncello tastes so much better than the store-bought varieties. Not only does it make for fine sipping after dinner, but its potent lemon flavor also makes it a good mixer in many cocktail recipes.

～ MAKES 2 LITERS ～

Lemon rinds (yellow part only) from 2 pounds lemons, preferably organic
1 liter 100-proof vodka
3 cups sugar
3 cups water

Combine the lemon peel and vodka in a large bowl. Cover and allow to steep for 1 week at room temperature. Combine the sugar and water in a large saucepan over medium heat and heat until the sugar has dissolved. Take off heat and allow to cool. Stir together the sugar syrup, and vodka mixture. Strain out the lemon peels from the vodka/sugar mixture and decant into 2 clean bottles with tight stoppers. Place the bottles in the refrigerator for 1 month, allowing the flavor to develop. Remove from the refrigerator, and store the limoncello in the freezer.

Serve icy cold in a shot or aperitif glass.

WHOLE PEACH DUMPLINGS *with* HONEY-CARAMEL SAUCE

Yet another classic from my grandmother's spiral-bound cookbook, this easy, virtually foolproof dessert was my children's favorite when they were young. I'd make it for them often in summer, but only if they did all their chores—and if they knew this was coming, the chores always got done!

What looks like a huge serving is, in reality, a single peach, pit, skin, and all, wrapped in pâte sucré. It is the sublime honey-caramel sauce drizzled over each pastry-wrapped peach that makes it indulgent. Of course, the quality of the peaches really makes a difference. They're most wonderful served warm, but they're still delicious at picnic temperature.

~ SERVES 6 ~

DUMPLINGS:

3	cups unbleached all-purpose flour
4	teaspoons granulated sugar
1½	teaspoons salt
1½	cups (3 sticks) cold unsalted butter, diced
6	tablespoons ice water
6	whole large ripe peaches (about 8 ounces each)
2	large egg yolks
6	teaspoons coarse sugar

HONEY-CARAMEL SAUCE:

1	cup powdered sugar
½	cup (1 stick) unsalted butter
⅓	cup honey
3	tablespoons heavy cream

TO PREPARE THE DUMPLINGS: Mix the flour, granulated sugar, and salt in a food processor. Add the butter and pulse just until the mixture resembles a coarse meal. Drizzle the ice water over the dough and pulse just until the dough pulls away from the sides of the bowl. Transfer the dough to a lightly floured work surface. Divide the dough into 7 equal pieces. Flatten each piece into a disc and wrap each disc in plastic. Refrigerate for at least 1 hour and up to 2 days.

Position the oven rack in the center of the oven and preheat the oven to 425°F. Line a heavy large baking sheet with parchment paper. Roll out 1 dough disc on a lightly floured work surface to a 9-inch round. Set 1 peach, stem side down, atop the center of the dough round. Fold the dough up and over the peach to encase it completely. Set the peach, stem end up, on the prepared baking sheet. Repeat with 5 of the remaining chilled dough discs and the remaining 5 peaches.

Beat the egg yolks in a small bowl to blend. Roll out the remaining dough disc until it is ⅛ inch thick and cut out leaf-shaped pieces. Brush the bottom of the leaves with the beaten egg yolks and set them atop the peach dumplings. Brush the dumplings with the remaining egg yolks and sprinkle each dumpling with 1 teaspoon of coarse sugar. Bake until the pastry is golden and the peaches are tender, about 25 minutes.

MEANWHILE, TO PREPARE THE HONEY-CARAMEL SAUCE: Stir the powdered sugar, butter, honey, and cream in a heavy medium saucepan over medium heat for 3 minutes, or until the mixture is well blended and smooth.

DO AHEAD: The dumplings and sauce can be made up to 8 hours ahead and served at room temperature. Cool them completely then store them in separate containers at room temperature. Transport the dumplings and sauce in a basket to your picnic.

Set 1 warm peach dumpling on each plate. Spoon the warm sauce over and around the dumplings and serve.

An Evening in Morocco

Some occasions are traditional, like Thanksgiving. Some are intimate, like a dinner party for close friends. But some occasions—perhaps a fiftieth birthday or a milestone anniversary—call for entertaining on a grander scale. This Moroccan menu is ideal for both a small and a large party, and it becomes more memorable if you set the stage with the décor, the music, and even your wardrobe.

My history with this party goes back to my early catering career. When a family asked if I could produce a lavish Moroccan-themed party, I agreed—even though I'd never been to Morocco, let alone thrown a party for 100. I set about researching the cuisine and the culture while planning with the clients, who had given me a substantial budget. We decided to have an esteemed Moroccan restaurant prepare the food, and I worked to make every detail perfect: hiring belly dancers, finding a live camel, renting 40-gallon palms from a movie studio, tenting the garden, hiring a staff, and securing elegant white Moroccan outfits for the family. I thought this would be the new direction for my new career: high-end event planner.

The night before the party, a rainstorm hit. The next day, the wonderful rental company worked with me in the pouring rain to salvage our set. The tent had to be lowered and made smaller so it wouldn't collapse under the weight of rainwater. We had to reconfigure the décor inside and out, and I had to cancel Mona the camel. I raced home to change into my Moroccan outfit, and when I returned, the guests were arriving. We'd pulled it off … and then the winds started howling, sending those 40-gallon palms into the tent walls. We scrambled to get everything secured, and after a too-long cocktail hour, everyone was ushered to their glittering tables, and a magnificent feast ensued. I had never been more exhausted in my life. After dinner, a friend asked me to dance; I took one step on the damp-with-rain dance floor, did a 360-degree flip (or so say witnesses), and was knocked out cold. Next thing I knew I woke up in the emergency room with a concussion. I literally knocked myself out for that party.

And yet the concussion did not spoil my love for this party—quite the contrary. With its savory-sweet flavors, seductive aromas, and romantic appeal, a Moroccan feast is always a hit. In fact, in 2005, when we decided to throw a street party for Julienne's twentieth anniversary, we returned to our Morocco theme. The city agreed to close the street, and we brought in huge papier-mâché camels, tents, belly dancers, tarot card readers, and buffets laden with bisteeya, couscous, tagines and roasted vegetables. Hundreds of people dressed in Moroccan attire filled the street, and everyone had a good time. Even if you make this Moroccan feast for ten instead of hundreds, it is guaranteed to be a memorable party.

MENU

Couscous with Cinnamon, Currants and Pine Nuts *137*

Roasted Cumin Carrots with Feta *139*

Lamb Tagine with Orange, Dried Apricots and Prunes *141*

Bisteeya with Chicken and Toasted Almonds *143*

Orange Slices with Cinnamon and Orange Flower Water Syrup *145*

COUSCOUS *with* CINNAMON, CURRANTS *and* PINE NUTS

What rice is to Asia and the potato is to the Americas, couscous is to North Africa. Couscous is actually a light pasta, made of crushed semolina and typically steamed in stock or water. In this recipe it's tossed with currants, vegetables, and spices, much like a pasta salad, and like a pasta salad, it's even better if you make it a day in advance. If you're not serving it with the cinnamony bisteeya (page 143), feel free to add a little more cinnamon here.

~ SERVES 6 TO 8 ~

⅔	cup dried currants
1	cup warm water
1½	cups chicken stock
1½	cups couscous
1½	cups diced celery
½	cup minced fresh parsley
½	cup toasted pine nuts
⅓	cup sliced green onions
¼	cup fresh lemon juice
1	teaspoon salt, plus more to taste
1	teaspoon freshly ground black pepper, plus more to taste
1	teaspoon ground cinnamon
½	cup olive oil

Place the currants and warm water in a small bowl and set aside until the currants plump, about 15 minutes. Drain and set the currants aside.

Bring the chicken stock to a boil in a large saucepan over high heat. Stir in the couscous, cover, and remove from the heat. Let the mixture stand until the stock is absorbed and the couscous is tender, about 5 minutes. Transfer the couscous to a large bowl. Mix in the celery, parsley, pine nuts, green onions, and plumped currants.

Whisk the lemon juice, 1 teaspoon of salt, 1 teaspoon of pepper, and cinnamon in a medium bowl. Gradually whisk in the oil. Drizzle the dressing over the couscous and toss to coat. Season the couscous to taste with more salt and pepper, if desired.

DO AHEAD: The couscous can be made 1 day ahead. Cover and refrigerate.

ROASTED CUMIN CARROTS *with* FETA

Roasting carrots brings out their sweetness, and adding aromatic cumin and tangy feta gives the dish balance and richness.

~ SERVES 6 TO 8 ~

2½   pounds large carrots, peeled, cut diagonally into ⅓-inch-thick slices
3   tablespoons olive oil
2   tablespoons ground cumin
2   garlic cloves, finely chopped
     Salt and freshly ground black pepper
⅔   cup minced fresh parsley
4   ounces feta cheese, coarsely crumbled

Position the oven rack in the center of the oven and preheat the oven to 425°F. Toss the carrots with the oil, cumin, and garlic. Arrange the carrot mixture in a single layer on a heavy large rimmed baking sheet. Sprinkle with salt and pepper. Roast the carrots, stirring occasionally, until they are golden and tender, about 30 minutes.

Transfer the carrot mixture to a bowl. Add the parsley and feta cheese to the warm carrots and toss to coat. Transfer to a platter and serve warm or at room temperature.

DO AHEAD: The carrots can be made up 6 hours ahead. After the carrots bake, set them aside at room temperature. Toss the carrots with the parsley and feta cheese just before serving.

LAMB TAGINE *with* ORANGE, DRIED APRICOTS *and* PRUNES

A tagine is a heavy clay pot with a domed lid that's been used for centuries in Morocco to slow-cook foods. Over time the stews that simmer in these pots also came to be called tagines. Handsome, though it is a traditional, a clay tagine is not necessary to make this richly flavorful dish—a modern Dutch oven will work just fine.

~ SERVES 6 TO 8 ~

1	cup dry sherry, divided
½	cup golden raisins
3	pounds boneless well-trimmed lamb shoulder, cut into 2-inch pieces
1½	cups fresh orange juice, divided
½	cup dried apricots
½	cup prunes
4	garlic cloves, minced
2	tablespoons olive oil
1	teaspoon salt, plus more for sprinkling
1	teaspoon freshly ground black pepper, plus more for sprinkling
1	yellow onion, chopped
2	teaspoons ground coriander
2	teaspoons ground cumin
2	teaspoons saffron
1	tablespoon unbleached all-purpose flour
½	cup dry red wine
3	ripe tomatoes (about 1¾ pounds total), cut into chunks
1	tablespoon toasted sesame seeds, for garnish

Combine ½ cup of the sherry and the raisins in a small bowl and set aside at room temperature for 2 hours.

Combine the lamb, 1 cup of orange juice, apricots, prunes, and garlic in a large bowl. Cover and refrigerate for 2 hours.

Position the oven rack in the center of the oven and pre-heat the oven to 350°F. Drain the marinade from the lamb; reserve the marinade. Pat the lamb dry with paper towels. Heat the oil in a heavy large Dutch oven or other ovenproof pot over medium-high heat. Sprinkle the lamb with salt and pepper. Working in 2 batches, add the lamb to the pot and cook until the lamb is brown all over, about 8 minutes. Transfer the lamb to a large bowl.

Add the onions to the same pot and sauté until brown, about 2 minutes. Stir in the coriander, cumin, and saffron.

Stir in the flour and cook for 1 minute. Add the sherry and raisin mixture, reserved marinade, wine, 1 teaspoon of salt, and 1 teaspoon of pepper. Return the lamb to the pot and stir to coat. Add the tomatoes. Bring to a simmer over medium-high heat. Cover the pot and place it in the oven until the meat is very tender, stirring occasionally, about 2 hours.

DO AHEAD: The tagine can be made up to this point 1 day ahead. Cool, then cover and refrigerate. Rewarm, covered, over low heat, stirring occasionally, before continuing.

Add the remaining ½ cup of orange juice and remaining ½ cup of sherry to the tagine. Return to a simmer. Sprinkle with the toasted sesame seeds and serve.

BISTEEYA *with* CHICKEN *and* TOASTED ALMONDS

Whether it's spelled "bisteeya" or "b'stilla" or "bistilla," the seductive and addictive blend of sweet and savory makes this dish one of the most beloved of Morocco's exports. Dating to the Middle Ages, this dish signifies special occasions, from weddings to holidays. It takes some time to prepare, but your guests will not forget it.

~ SERVES 6 TO 8 ~

FILLING:

3	tablespoons unsalted butter
1	onion, chopped
2½	cups diced cooked chicken breasts
	(from 2 boneless skinless chicken breasts)
2	teaspoons ground cinnamon
1	teaspoon ground ginger
1	teaspoon turmeric
1½	teaspoons salt, plus more to taste
½	teaspoon freshly ground black pepper, plus more to taste
1	cup sliced almonds, toasted
¾	cup chopped fresh parsley
3	extra-large eggs
¼	cup chicken broth

ASSEMBLY:

1½	tablespoons sugar
1½	teaspoons ground cinnamon
6	fresh or frozen phyllo sheets, thawed if frozen (each about 17 x 12 inches)
6	tablespoons (¾ stick; about) unsalted butter, melted

TO PREPARE THE FILLING: Melt the butter in a heavy large sauté pan over medium heat. Add the onions and sauté until they are soft, about 8 minutes. Add the chicken and sprinkle with the cinnamon, ginger, turmeric, 1½ teaspoons of salt, and ½ teaspoon of pepper. Stir in the almonds and parsley. Whisk the eggs and chicken broth in a large bowl over a saucepan of simmering water until the mixture thickens and begins to curdle, about 2 minutes. Stir into the chicken mixture. Cool completely.

DO AHEAD: The filling can be made 1 day ahead. Cover and refrigerate.

continued on next page

TO ASSEMBLE THE BISTEEYA: Position the oven rack in the center of the oven and preheat the oven to 350°F. Mix the granulated sugar and cinnamon in a small bowl. Stack 2 sheets of phyllo and lay them in an 8- to 9-inch pie pan. Brush the top phyllo sheet with some of the melted butter and sprinkle with some of the cinnamon sugar. Lay 2 more sheets of phyllo on top, arranging these sheets in the opposite direction of the first layer in order to create a cross pattern. Brush with more butter and sprinkle with more cinnamon sugar. Repeat with the remaining 2 sheets of phyllo, arranging them in the same direction as the first 2 sheets of phyllo. Brush with more butter and sprinkle with more cinnamon sugar. Spoon the chicken mixture into the phyllo-lined pan. Gather the edges of the phyllo and fold them over the filling, raising the edges to create a decorative border and allowing the filling to be seen in the center. Brush the phyllo border lightly with the remaining butter and sprinkle with the remaining cinnamon sugar.

Bake until the phyllo is golden brown, about 45 minutes, covering the phyllo border with foil after 30 minutes if it begins to brown too much. Remove from the oven and serve warm.

ORANGE SLICES *with* CINNAMON *and* ORANGE FLOWER WATER SYRUP

This syrup is out of this world! It's also quite versatile—you can drizzle it over strawberries, wedges of fresh peaches, fresh sliced figs, or almost any fruit. If you don't have time to marinate the oranges in advance, don't worry—they're still terrific when served right after the syrup is added.

~ SERVES 6 TO 8~

2	cups freshly squeeze orange juice
½	cup granulated sugar
½	cup orange flower water
6	cinnamon sticks
8	large oranges
2	teaspoons powdered sugar, for garnish
1	teaspoon ground cinnamon, for garnish
8	mint sprigs, for garnish

Combine the orange juice, granulated sugar, orange flower water, and cinnamon sticks in a heavy medium saucepan. Boil over medium-high heat until slightly syrupy and reduced to 1 cup, about 10 minutes. Cool, and discard the cinnamon sticks.

Cut the peel and pith from the oranges. Cut each orange into 6 rounds. Arrange the orange slices on a platter, overlapping them slightly. Pour half of the cooled syrup over the oranges. Cover and marinate in the refrigerator for 2 hours.

DO AHEAD: The syrup can be made up to 3 days ahead; cover and refrigerate. The oranges can marinate up to 8 hours before serving.

Combine the powdered sugar and ground cinnamon in a small sieve and lightly sift it over the oranges. Garnish with mint sprigs and serve immediately.

A Harvest Feast

After the relaxed, open days of summer, with vacations, summer jobs, and backyard barbecues, late fall brings a focus on home, hearth, and tradition. Most of us think of Thanksgiving when it comes to fall feasts, and indeed, it is the focal point for most American families. For three decades, my family of up to forty has gathered for a weekend Thanksgiving celebration on the beach in La Jolla, centered around a huge potluck turkey dinner on the sand. That's our tradition, and every family has its own.

There's more to fall entertaining, however, than one day of turkey. In fact, fall is my favorite season to both cook and entertain, and there are always occasions to mark: a tailgate party, or Octoberfest, or just an excuse to rekindle your fireplace. I love the foods that come into season around October, and I also love the flavor combinations that work so well when there's a chill in the air: pork with dried fruit; savory braised cabbage and gratin potato dishes; green salads enlivened with fall fruits; and rich, warm desserts, like my mother's Steamed Persimmon Pudding with Sherry Sabayon.

One of my Thanksgiving traditions with my children and now my grandchildren works well for any fall gathering. To decorate the table, I take a few children on a hunt around the neighborhood for autumn leaves, and they have fun looking for the largest, most colorful ones. We add a few gourds, pomegranates, and pumpkins and dust everything with a little gold spray paint. Then we all arrange the golden leaves, pumpkins, pomegranates and gourds, interspersed with lots of candles, on our harvest table. The cost is negligible, and the look never fails to delight guests—and set the stage for a meal of robust fall flavors.

MENU

Harvest Salad with Pears, Dried Figs, Baby Spinach and Cider Vinaigrette *149*

Mustard Roasted Pork Tenderloin
with Dried Apricots, Orange and Ginger Sauce *151*

Braised Red Cabbage with Apples, Golden Raisins and Caraway Seeds *153*

Potato, Gruyère and Fennel Gratin *155*

Steamed Persimmon Pudding with Sherry Sabayon *156*

HARVEST SALAD *with* PEARS, DRIED FIGS, BABY SPINACH *and* CIDER VINAIGRETTE

Nothing connotes fall more than pears, rich toasted nuts, and dried figs—and this dish is one of the reasons I love fall so much.

~ SERVES 6 TO 8 ~

CIDER VINAIGRETTE:

3	tablespoons apple cider vinegar
1	teaspoon Dijon mustard
1	garlic clove, minced
½	teaspoon sugar
⅓	cup extra-virgin olive oil
	Salt and freshly ground black pepper

SALAD:

½	cup pecans
12	ounces fresh baby spinach leaves
2	red Anjou pears, cored, cut into ½-inch pieces (skin on)
1	small red onion, very thinly sliced
¾	cup dried Black Mission figs, cut into ½-inch pieces or halved
1	tablespoon fresh lemon juice
4	ounces Gorgonzola cheese, coarsely crumbled

TO PREPARE THE CIDER VINAIGRETTE: Whisk the vinegar, mustard, garlic, and sugar in a large bowl to blend. Gradually whisk in the oil to blend well. Season the vinaigrette to taste with salt and pepper.

TO PREPARE THE SALAD: Position the oven rack in the center of the oven and preheat the oven to 350°F. Place the pecans on a baking sheet and roast them until they are fragrant and golden brown in the center, stirring occasionally to ensure they brown evenly, about 10 minutes. Set aside to cool, then coarsely chop the pecans.

DO AHEAD: The vinaigrette and pecans can be prepared 1 day ahead. Cover and refrigerate the vinaigrette. Whisk the vinaigrette before using. Store the pecans in an airtight container at room temperature.

Toss the spinach in a large bowl with enough vinaigrette to coat. Mound the spinach on plates. Toss the pears, onion, figs, and lemon juice in a medium bowl, then scatter the pear mixture over the salads. Sprinkle with the pecans and cheese, and serve immediately.

MUSTARD ROASTED PORK TENDERLOIN
with DRIED APRICOTS, ORANGE *and* GINGER SAUCE

Pork tenderloins are very tender and cook quickly—two good reasons why everyone loves them. (And for bonus points, they're low in fat.) The savory-sweet sauce takes even less time to prepare than the pork, so this dish works for even the busiest night.

~ SERVES 8~

PORK:

2	1-pound pork tenderloins
	Salt and freshly ground black pepper
2	tablespoons olive oil, divided
6	garlic cloves, peeled
½	cup (lightly packed) fresh parsley leaves
1½	tablespoons fennel seeds
¼	cup coarse Dijon mustard

SAUCE:

1	cup ruby Port
½	cup chicken stock
½	cup dried apricots, finely diced or halved
½	cup dried cranberries
⅔	cup fresh orange juice
¼	cup red currant jelly
1½	tablespoons fresh lemon juice
1	teaspoon minced peeled fresh ginger
1	teaspoon ground ginger
¼	teaspoon salt
1	tablespoon cornstarch
1	tablespoon water
2	tablespoons (¼ stick) cold unsalted butter, cut into pieces

TO PREPARE THE PORK: Using a sharp knife, remove the sinew from the pork tenderloins. Sprinkle the pork with salt and pepper. Heat 1 tablespoon of the oil in a heavy large skillet over high heat. Add the pork tenderloins and cook just until brown on all sides, about 3 minutes. Transfer the pork to a heavy large rimmed baking sheet and set aside to cool slightly.

Mince the garlic in a mini food processor. Add the parsley, fennel seeds, and the remaining 1 tablespoon of oil and blend until the parsley is finely chopped (most of the fennel

continued on next page

seeds will remain whole). Spread the mustard over the pork, then coat the pork with the herb mixture. Cover and refrigerate for at least 8 hours and up to 1 day.

Preheat the oven to 450°F. Roast the pork until an instant-read thermometer inserted into the center of the meat registers 140°F to 145°F, about 15 minutes. Let the pork stand for 5 minutes.

MEANWHILE, TO PREPARE THE SAUCE: Combine the Port, stock, apricots, and cranberries in a heavy medium saucepan and boil over medium-high heat for 1 minute. Add the orange juice, jelly, lemon juice, fresh ginger, ground ginger, and salt. Stir the sauce until the jelly dissolves, about 2 minutes. Whisk the cornstarch and water in a small bowl to blend, then whisk the cornstarch mixture into the sauce. Simmer until the juices thicken, whisking constantly, about 3 minutes. Whisk in any accumulated pan juices from the pork. Remove the pan from the heat and whisk in the butter.

Transfer the pork to a carving board and cut the pork into thin slices. Arrange the pork slices on plates. Spoon the sauce over and serve immediately.

BRAISED RED CABBAGE
with APPLES, GOLDEN RAISINS *and* CARAWAY SEEDS

This cabbage side dish boasts sweet and sour flavors that complement the pork and potatoes beautifully. It is even better the next day.

~ SERVES 6 TO 8 ~

5	tablespoons unsalted butter
1	medium red onion, chopped
1	garlic clove, chopped
2	large Fuji apples, cored, cut into ½-inch cubes (skin on)
2	tablespoons balsamic vinegar
2	tablespoons (packed) golden brown sugar
½	cup apple cider
½	cup golden raisins
1	tablespoon caraway seeds
1	tablespoon Dijon mustard
¾	teaspoon kosher salt, plus more to taste
¾	teaspoon freshly ground black pepper, plus more to taste
1	head red cabbage (about 2 pounds), cored, thinly sliced

Melt the butter in a heavy large pot over medium heat. Add the onion and garlic and sauté until tender, about 8 minutes. Add the apples, vinegar, and brown sugar and sauté until the apples soften, about 8 minutes. Mix in the cider, raisins, caraway seeds, mustard, ¾ teaspoon of salt, and ¾ teaspoon of pepper. Stir in the cabbage. The cabbage will fill the pot when it is first added, but will soften and shrink down as it cooks. Cover and simmer until most of the liquid evaporates and the cabbage softens, stirring often for the first 40 minutes ,then stirring frequently during the last 5 minutes, about 45 minutes total. Season to taste with more salt and pepper.

DO AHEAD: The cabbage can be made up to 2 days ahead. Cool completely, then cover and refrigerate. Rewarm the cabbage mixture in a heavy large saucepan, covered, over medium heat, stirring occasionally.

POTATO, GRUYÈRE *and* FENNEL GRATIN

The sometimes-powerful anise flavor of fennel mellows considerably when sautéed in this recipe, lending a subtly tangy sweetness that complements the cheese and cream. You can speed up your prep time by using a vegetable slicer to thinly slice the potatoes— but prepare them just before they are baked, so they don't turn brown from sitting around.

~ SERVES 6 TO 8 ~

1	tablespoon olive oil
1	tablespoon unsalted butter
3	fennel bulbs, halved lengthwise, then thinly sliced crosswise
1	onion, chopped
3	pounds russet potatoes (about 3 large), peeled, cut into ⅛-inch-thick slices
2½	cups (lightly packed; about 8 ounces) grated Gruyère cheese
1	cup heavy cream
1	cup whole milk
1	teaspoon kosher salt
½	teaspoon freshly ground black pepper

Heat the oil and butter in a heavy large sauté pan over medium-high heat until the butter melts. Add the fennel and onions and sauté until tender, about 15 minutes. Set aside to cool slightly.

DO AHEAD: The fennel mixture can be prepared 1 day ahead. Cool completely, then cover and refrigerate.

Position the oven rack in the center of the oven and pre-heat the oven to 350°F. Butter a 13 x 9 x 2-inch baking dish. Arrange one-third of the potato slices in the baking dish. Stir the cheese, cream, milk, salt, pepper, and cooled fennel mixture in a large bowl. Scatter one-third of the cheese mixture over the potatoes. Repeat layering 2 more times with the remaining potatoes and cheese mixture. Cover with foil and bake until the potatoes are almost tender, about 1 hour. Uncover and continue baking until the potatoes are tender and the top is golden, about 20 minutes longer. Set aside to cool slightly, about 15 minutes, before serving.

STEAMED PERSIMMON PUDDING *with* SHERRY SABAYON

Using very ripe Hachiya persimmons is the key to this recipe —Hachiya are the elongated variety that soften as they ripen, while the squat, round Fuyu remain firm when ripe, and therefore won't work. The rich Sherry Sabayon (see the following recipe) pairs perfectly with this moist, dense, pudding-like cake. This is another one of my mother's favorite recipes that she made with such pride in her double boiler and served at Thanksgiving and Christmas.

~ SERVES 8~

	Nonstick cooking spray
4 to 5	very ripe Hachiya persimmons (about 1¼ pounds total)
1	cup unbleached all-purpose flour
1½	teaspoons baking soda
1	teaspoon ground cinnamon
½	teaspoon salt
1	cup sugar
1	extra-large egg, beaten to blend
2	tablespoons (¼ stick) unsalted butter, melted
1	cup golden raisins
½	cup buttermilk
1	cup walnuts, chopped
	Sherry Sabayon (see following recipe)

Position the oven rack in the center of the oven and preheat the oven to 350°F. Spray a 4-cup metal pudding mold with nonstick cooking spray. Tear the persimmons open and scrape the flesh into a medium-mesh sieve set over a large bowl. Using a rubber spatula, press the flesh through the sieve and into the bowl (discard the solids). You should have 1 cup of puree.

Whisk the flour, baking soda, cinnamon, and salt in a medium bowl to blend; set aside. Whisk the sugar into the persimmon puree to blend. Whisk in the egg and melted butter. Stir in the raisins. Whisk in the flour mixture, alternating with the buttermilk. Stir in the walnuts. Pour the batter into the prepared mold.

Cover with a lid or foil and set the mold in a 2-quart soufflé dish. Add enough cold water to come halfway up the sides of the mold. Bake until the pudding is set near the center, about 2 hours. Remove the mold from the soufflé dish. Uncover the pudding and invert the mold onto a rack until the pudding cools slightly, about 15 minutes. Remove the mold.

DO AHEAD: The pudding can be made up to this point 1 month ahead. Cool the pudding completely, then wrap it with foil and freeze. Thaw the pudding then rewarm it (wrapped in foil) in a 250°F oven for 20 to 30 minutes.

Cut the warm pudding into wedges and transfer to plates. Spoon the Sherry Sabayon atop the pudding, and serve immediately.

SHERRY SABAYON

A sabayon is a French custard made with wine, eggs, and sugar. This one is made ethereally light by the addition of meringue and whipped cream. When you first make it, it will resemble whipped cream, but after it sits a few hours, it will loosen up and become more like a light custard sauce—either way, it is delicious. If you're squeamish about eating raw egg whites, leave them out and just use the whipped cream— the sabayon will still be plenty fluffy. This is also wonderful served simply with fresh berries.

MAKES ABOUT 5 CUPS

½   cup sherry

2   extra-large eggs, separated

¾   cup powdered sugar, sifted, divided

1   cup chilled heavy cream

Whisk the sherry, egg yolks, and ¼ cup of the powdered sugar in a large bowl to blend. Set the bowl over a saucepan of simmering water (do not allow the bottom of the bowl to touch the water). Whisk rapidly until the mixture is thick and foamy and a thermometer inserted into the mixture registers 160°F, about 1 minute. Refrigerate the sabayon until it is cold, whisking occasionally, about 15 minutes.

Using an electric mixer with a clean whisk attachment, beat the egg whites in another large bowl until frothy. Gradually add the remaining ½ cup of powdered sugar, beating until the mixture is stiff. Fold the meringue into the sabayon. Beat the cream in the same large bowl until thick and firm peaks form when the beater is lifted (you do not need to clean the beater or bowl before beating the cream). Fold the cream into the sabayon.

DO AHEAD: The sabayon can be made 8 hours ahead. Cover and refrigerate.

A Winter Celebration

Even before making a name among my friends for my Brie en croute, I was a baker known for my gingerbread houses. I made them with my children, I made them for my friends, and eventually I taught classes at home and for UCLA Extension on making gingerbread houses. Creating these fanciful houses came to define the holiday season for me.

I no longer spend untold hours crafting dozens of peppermint roofs and gingerbread-man walkways, but I still look forward to the traditions of the winter season and to making at least one gingerbread house. My family now holds an annual gingerbread-house-making session on a Sunday in early December, and this gathering of my grandchildren and all the cousins has turned into another cherished tradition.

For me, hosting a winter dinner party means bringing together friends and family for a sit-down celebration that's more elegant than gatherings at other times of the year. There's something about the longer, colder nights and the religious and cultural traditions of the season that call for dressing up, setting a beautiful table, and preparing a special meal that takes some effort and showcases excellent ingredients.

This Winter Celebration menu is ideal for a beautiful Christmas Eve or holiday-season dinner. It starts with succulent seared scallops paired with black rice galettes and finished with a blood-orange sauce. Next comes an intermezzo of my grandmother's cranberry ice, which my family has served at every Thanksgiving and Christmas for years. For a main course, you'll enjoy a rich Muscovy duck breast with a spiced pomegranate sauce. For a side dish, I make a flaky phyllo cup filled with a puree of celery root topped with a frizzle of fried sage. To conclude, there's a decadent chocolate-cranberry torte garnished with edible gold leaf.

A meal like this may invite a certain elegance of dress and décor, but that doesn't mean you have to spend a lot of money. Crisp table linens, fresh candles, and some beautiful flowers and holiday greenery are all you need to set the stage for a memorable evening.

MENU

Seared Scallops with Blood Orange Sauce and Black Rice Gallettes *161*

Cranberry Ice *163*

Muscovy Duck Breasts with Spiced Pomegranate Sauce and Dried Cherries *164*

Phyllo Cups with Celery Root Puree *165*

Chocolate Cranberry Torte with Frosted Cranberries and Gold Leaf *167*

SEARED SCALLOPS
with **BLOOD ORANGE SAUCE** *and* **BLACK RICE GALETTES**

I love the contrast of textures, colors and flavors in this elegant dish that I created after hours of experimenting. It combines the deep, nutty taste of short-grained black rice (sometimes called "forbidden rice") with tender scallops and the sweet-tangy sauce of orange and Muscat. If you don't have Muscat handy, you can substitute a sweet Riesling or Gewürztraminer.

~ SERVES 6 ~

BLACK RICE GALETTES:

3	tablespoons butter, divided
½	cup finely diced onion
½	cup uncooked black rice
½	teaspoon salt
½	cup dry white wine
1½	cups chicken stock
1	extra-large egg yolk
	Nonstick cooking spray
1	tablespoon olive oil

BLOOD ORANGE SAUCE:

4	blood oranges
2	cups sweet Muscat wine or other sweet white wine
¼	cup finely chopped shallots
4	tablespoons (½ stick) chilled unsalted butter, cut into pieces
	salt and freshly ground pepper

SCALLOPS:

6	jumbo scallops (each about 2 inches in diameter)
2	tablespoons chopped fresh parsley
1	tablespoon chopped fresh tarragon
2	tablespoons olive oil
	Microgreens, for garnish
3	blood oranges, segmented

FOR THE BLACK RICE GALETTES: Melt 2 tablespoons of butter in a heavy 1-quart saucepan over medium heat. Add the onions and sauté until they are translucent, about 4 minutes. Add the rice and sauté until it is fragrant, about 1 minute. Stir in the salt. Add the wine and simmer until it is reduced by half, about 2 minutes. Add the chicken stock. Bring the liquid to a boil, then reduce the heat to medium-low. Cover and simmer gently without stirring until the rice is tender and the liquid has evaporated, about 55

continued on next page

minutes. Cool completely. Mix in the egg yolk.

Line a baking sheet with parchment paper. Spray a 2½-inch-diameter ring mold with nonstick cooking spray. Set the mold on top of the parchment paper. Fill the ring mold with 3 tablespoons of rice, pressing to compact and form a ½-inch-thick galette. Remove the ring mold and repeat to form 6 galettes total. Cover and refrigerate.

DO AHEAD: The galettes can be prepared up to this point 1 day ahead. Keep refrigerated.

FOR THE BLOOD ORANGE SAUCE: Using a microplane grater, grate 3 tablespoons of zest from the oranges, then squeeze 1 cup of juice from the blood oranges. Combine the juice, zest, wine, and shallots in a heavy medium saucepan. Bring the mixture to a boil over high heat. Reduce the heat to low and simmer uncovered until the liquid is reduced to ¼ cup, about 25 minutes. Remove the saucepan from the heat. Add the butter 1 piece at a time, whisking constantly until the sauce is well blended. Season the sauce to taste with salt and pepper. Strain the sauce through a fine-meshed strainer into a medium bowl. Set the bowl over a saucepan of simmering water to keep the sauce warm.

TO PREPARE THE SCALLOPS AND ASSEMBLE: Heat 1 tablespoon of oil and the remaining 1 tablespoon of butter in a heavy large frying pan over medium heat. Fry the galettes, 3 at a time, until crisp and heated through, turning once, about 2 minutes on each side. Drain on paper towels.

Meanwhile, remove the tough side muscle attached to each scallop. Mix the parsley and tarragon on a small plate, then dip the tops and bottoms of the scallops in the herbs to coat (do not coat the sides of the scallops). Heat 2 tablespoons of oil in a heavy large skillet over high heat. Add the scallops and cook until golden brown on the bottom, about 3 minutes. Using a metal spatula, turn the scallops over and cook until golden brown on the bottom and still translucent in the center, about 3 minutes longer. Scallops become rubbery when overcooked, so they should be a bit translucent in the center when done.

Place 1 rice galette on each of 6 warm plates and top each with 1 scallop. Top the scallops with a small mound of microgreens. Arrange the orange segments around the galettes. Drizzle with the sauce and serve.

CRANBERRY ICE

My grandmother served this as an intermezzo at every holiday meal, and decades later, my family still adores it and wouldn't consider a Thanksgiving or Christmas without it. We make this several days before our celebration dinner in order for the ice to set.

~ SERVES 6~

1	12-ounce package fresh cranberries (about 3½ cups)
2	cups water
1½	cups sugar
1	teaspoon finely grated orange zest
½	cup freshly squeezed orange juice
¼	cup cream sherry
1	large egg white
½	cup blanched slivered almonds, toasted

Combine the cranberries and water in a heavy medium saucepan. Cook over medium heat until the cranberries pop, stirring occasionally, about 5 minutes.

Drain the cranberry mixture through a strainer, reserving the liquid in a 2-cup liquid measuring cup; set the cranberries aside. Add enough water to the reserved cranberry cooking liquid to equal 2 cups of liquid total. Return the cranberry liquid to the saucepan. Add the sugar and bring to a boil, stirring to dissolve the sugar.

Meanwhile, puree the cranberries and orange zest in the food processor until pureed. Whisk the cranberry puree into the cranberry liquid. Strain the cranberry mixture through a fine-meshed sieve into a 13 x 9 x 2-inch baking pan. Set the cranberry liquid aside to cool, about 1 hour.

Stir the orange juice and sherry into the cooled cranberry mixture. Cover and freeze until the cranberry mixture is partially frozen and thick, stirring occasionally, about 3 hours.

Using an electric mixer with the whisk attachment, beat the egg white in a clean large bowl until soft peaks form when the whisk is lifted from the egg white. Fold the egg white into the partially frozen cranberry mixture, then fold in the almonds. Cover and freeze overnight, stirring occasionally.

Serve in dessert glasses.

MUSCOVY DUCK BREASTS
with SPICED POMEGRANATE SAUCE *and* DRIED CHERRIES

The red wine sauce in this dish is redolent with many wonderful holiday flavors—cinnamon, cloves, and pomegranate—all of which complement the duck. Because it's Christmas, I splurge and cook more duck than is strictly necessary, so each guest receives prime slices … no end pieces for my friends! Look for Muscovy duck breasts, which are typically thicker and meatier; you'll find them at quality butcher shops, gourmet markets, and online.

~ SERVES 6 ~

SPICED POMEGRANATE SAUCE:

2	cups Merlot or other dry red wine
¾	cup pure pomegranate juice (such as Pom)
¾	cup ruby Port
¼	cup finely chopped shallots
1	cinnamon stick
6	whole cloves
½	cup dried tart cherries, divided
4	tablespoons (½ stick) unsalted butter, cut into small pieces

DUCK:

3	1-pound boneless Muscovy duck breast halves with skin
	Salt and freshly ground black pepper
2	tablespoons chopped fresh thyme

FOR THE SAUCE: Combine the Merlot, pomegranate juice, Port, shallots, cinnamon stick, cloves, and half of the cherries in a heavy medium saucepan. Simmer over medium-high heat until reduced to ¾ cup, about 45 minutes. Strain the sauce into a small saucepan (you should have a scant ⅔ cup of sauce). Whisk in the butter. Stir the remaining cherries into the sauce. Cover and keep warm.

MEANWHILE, TO PREPARE THE DUCK: Preheat the oven to 400°F. Score the skin of the duck breasts with a sharp knife and season with salt, pepper, and thyme. Be careful not to cut into the meat. Place 2 of the duck breasts, skin side down, in a heavy large skillet. Cook over medium heat until the skin is crisp and brown, about 8 minutes. Transfer the duck breasts to a heavy rimmed baking sheet, fat side up. Pour off the excess pan drippings. Repeat with the remaining duck breasts.

Transfer the baking sheet to the oven and roast the duck breasts until an instant-read thermometer inserted into the thickest part of meat registers 140°F, about 15 minutes. Transfer the duck breasts to a carving board and let rest for 10 minutes to allow the juices to remain in the duck.

When ready to serve, cut the duck breasts on a diagonal into ¼-inch-thick slices and divide among 6 plates. Spoon the sauce over the duck breasts and serve.

PHYLLO CUPS *with* CELERY ROOT PUREE

Phyllo cups are wonderful vehicles for all sorts of fillings, and they make elegant accompaniments to roasts, prime rib, and game. To accompany the richly seasoned Muscovy duck entrée, I like to fill the cups with a straightforward celery-root puree that won't fight for attention on the plate.

To work with phyllo, give yourself lots of room, be sure to have everything ready before you unwrap the pastry sheets, and keep the sheets covered so they don't dry out.

~ SERVES 6~

PHYLLO CUPS:

4	fresh or frozen phyllo sheets, thawed if frozen (each about 17 x 12 inches)
3	tablespoons (about) unsalted butter, melted

CELERY ROOT PUREE:

6	tablespoons (¾ stick) unsalted butter, cut into chunks
2½	pounds celery roots (about 3), peeled, cut into 1-inch chunks
1	garlic clove, coarsely chopped
½	cup heavy cream
1	teaspoon kosher salt
⅛	teaspoon freshly ground white pepper
½	cup canola oil
6	fresh sage leaves
2	tablespoons chopped fresh chives

TO MAKE THE PHYLLO CUPS: Position the oven rack in the center of the oven and preheat the oven to 350°F. Set the stack of phyllo aside on a work surface and cover completely with plastic wrap. Remove 1 phyllo sheet and lay it on the work surface. Brush the phyllo sheet with some melted butter, then top with 3 more sheets of phyllo, brushing each with butter.

Cut the buttered stack of phyllo into six 4½-to 5-inch squares. Line each of six ½-cup muffin cups with a phyllo square. Bake the cups until golden, about 10 minutes, then cool completely in the pan on a rack.

MEANWHILE, TO MAKE THE CELERY ROOT PUREE: Melt the butter in a heavy large sauté pan over medium-low heat. Add the celery roots and garlic and stir to coat with the butter. Cover and cook until the celery root is pale golden and tender enough to mash with a spoon, stirring occasionally, about 30 minutes. Stir in the cream, salt, and pepper. Transfer the mixture to a food processor and blend until smooth, about 2 minutes.

Heat the oil in a heavy small sauté pan over medium heat. Add the sage leaves and fry until they are crisp, about 2 minutes. Using a slotted spoon, transfer the sage leaves to paper towels to drain the excess oil.

DO AHEAD: The phyllo cups, the celery root puree, and the fried sage leaves can be made 1 day ahead. Cover the phyllo cups in the muffin pan and wrap the pan loosely with plastic wrap. Store the sage leaves in an airtight container. Store the phyllo cups and fried sage leaves at room temperature. Transfer the celery root puree to a bowl, cool, then cover and refrigerate. Before serving, set the bowl of puree over a saucepan of simmering water and stir until it is heated through. Bake the phyllo cups in a 300°F oven until warm, about 5 minutes.

TO SERVE: Set 1 warm phyllo cup on each of 6 plates. Stir the chives into the warm puree. Spoon the puree into each phyllo cup, garnish with the fried sage leaves, and serve immediately.

CHOCOLATE CRANBERRY TORTE
with FROSTED CRANBERRIES *and* GOLD LEAF

Thanks to the minimal amount of flour and generous amount of chocolate, this glazed torte is denser and fudgier than most frosted cakes. And the glaze is perfect not just for this dessert but also for many others—dip the tops of cupcakes into it, pour it over a pan of brownies, or drizzle it over your favorite ice cream. You can find edible gold leaf online and at some cookware stores.

~ SERVES 12 ~

TORTE:

	Nonstick cooking spray
½	cup blanched slivered almonds
¼	cup unbleached all-purpose flour
1	16-ounce can whole-berry cranberry sauce
½	teaspoon almond extract
7	ounces fine-quality semisweet chocolate (about 54% cacao), coarsely chopped
½	cup (1 stick) unsalted butter
½	cup sugar
3	extra-large eggs, separated
	Pinch of salt

GL AZE:

6	ounces fine-quality bittersweet chocolate (56% to 60% cacao), finely chopped
½	cup heavy cream
2	tablespoons (¼ stick) unsalted butter
1	tablespoon water

Frosted Cranberries, for garnish (see following recipe)
Edible gold leaf, for garnish

TO PREPARE THE TORTE: Position the oven rack in the bottom third of the oven and preheat the oven to 350°F. Spray a 9-inch-diameter springform pan with cooking spray. Line the bottom with parchment paper and spray the paper with the cooking spray. Pulse the nuts in a food processor until they are finely chopped and resemble a coarse cornmeal. Add the flour and blend until the nuts are finely ground. Grinding the nuts with the flour helps prevent the nuts from clumping together and forming an almond butter. Set the almond-flour mixture aside.

Gently stir the cranberry sauce with the almond extract in a small bowl to loosen. Combine the chocolate and butter in a medium metal bowl. Set the bowl over a saucepan of

continued on next page

simmering water and stir until melted and smooth. Remove from the heat and set aside until just cool to the touch, about 10 minutes.

Using an electric mixer with the paddle attachment, beat the sugar, egg yolks, and salt in a large bowl until thick and light, about 5 minutes. With the mixer on low speed, add the almond-flour mixture, beating just until blended. Using a large rubber spatula, fold in the melted chocolate-butter mixture just until blended. Fold in the reserved cranberry sauce with the almond extract.

Using an electric mixer on medium speed with a clean, dry whisk attachment, beat the egg whites in another large bowl until thick soft peaks form, about 3 minutes. Using the large rubber spatula, gently fold the whites into the batter. Immediately pour the batter into the prepared pan, using the rubber spatula to smooth the surface gently.

Bake until the torte is set around the edges and begins to pull away from the sides of the pan, about 48 minutes. Unlike most cakes that are baked until set in the center and until a toothpick comes out clean when inserted into the center, the center of this torte actually still moves slightly when the pan is gently shaken, and because of the high amount of chocolate and butter in this torte, it will set as it cools.

Cool the torte completely in the pan, then refrigerate until it is cold, at least 1 hour. As the cake cools it with fall slightly in the center. Run a small knife around the pan sides to loosen the cake from the pan. Release the pan sides from the torte and invert it onto a cooling rack (the top of the torte will now be on the bottom). Remove the pan bottom and parchment paper from the torte.

TO MAKE THE GLAZE: Stir the chocolate, cream, butter, and water in a heavy small saucepan over medium-low heat until melted and smooth.

Place waxed paper under the rack and pour all of the glaze over the torte. Tilt the torte to allow the glaze to cover the top completely, then cover all of the sides. Use a long metal offset spatula to help spread the glaze. Lift the wire rack and tap it gently to smooth the glaze on the sides and allow the excess glaze to run off. Set the torte aside until the glaze is cool. Transfer the torte to a cake platter.

DO AHEAD: The glazed torte can be made 1 day ahead. Cover with a cake dome and refrigerate.

Just before serving, decorate the top of the torte with the frosted cranberries and garnish with the gold leaf.

FROSTED CRANBERRIES

These are great not only with the chocolate torte—they add color and a tart sweetness to trifles, bûches de Noël, cheesecakes, even cupcakes. A sprinkling of these will make almost any dessert look fancy.

1   **extra-large egg white**
2   **cups fresh cranberries, washed, dried well**
⅓   **cup sugar**

Line a baking sheet with waxed paper. Stir the egg white in a small bowl to loosen. Dip each cranberry in to the unbeaten egg white to coat lightly, then drop the cranberry in the sugar, tossing to coat completely. Using a fork, lift the cranberry from the sugar and place it on the waxed paper and set aside at room temperature until dried. Do not refrigerate the frosted cranberries as this will cause the sugar coating to melt.

DO AHEAD: The frosted cranberries can be made 1 day ahead. Store the cranberries in an airtight container at room temperature.

Contributors

Joseph Shuldiner
ART DIRECTOR

Joseph Shuldiner has been involved in the field of publication design for more than twenty years. He was the founding creative director of *Distinction* magazine, published by the *Los Angeles Times*. He is currently a nationally exhibited fine artist as well as an independent art director and consultant specializing in the fields of magazine, and book production, design and photography. He is the designer of *EAT: Los Angeles* and co-designer of *Cooking with Café Pasqual's*. Joseph is thrilled to have been a part of the *Celebrating with Julienne* creative team and wishes to thank Sue Campoy for her vision, her patience, and her perseverance (and for keeping him extremely well fed).

www.josephshuldiner.com

Emily Brooke Sandor
PHOTOGRAPHER

Emily Brooke Sandor is a food, travel, and still life photographer based in Los Angeles. Her work has appeared in *Gourmet*, *Health*, *C*, and *Garden Design* magazine, among other publications here and abroad. She has received the prestigious Lucie award for both her food, and her travel photography. The Julienne cookbook is Emily's fourth book. Previous books include *Zen Flowers*, *Pops! Icy Treats for Everyone*, and *Douro en Objectiva*, a collaborative book project for the Portuguese Tourism Board about the Douro River region of Northern Portugal, due out in summer 2009.

www.sandorphotography.com

Rochelle Palermo
RECIPE EDITOR

Rochelle Palermo has worked on such books as Ludo LeFerve's *Crave* and Curtis Stone's *Relax with Curtis* and is a regular contributor to *Bon Appetit* magazine. She was the recipe co-creator and writer for Giada De Laurentiis' shows *Everyday Italian* and *Giada's Family Dinners*. Rochelle was a contributing writer for *The Bon Appetit Cookbook* as well as *Fast, Easy, Fresh*.

rochellepalermo@earthlink.net

Colleen Dunn Bates
WRITER

Colleen Dunn Bates is a longtime L.A. writer, editor, and book publisher with a particular passion for food. She is the editor and publisher of *EAT: Los Angeles*, the publisher of such books as *Hometown Pasadena* and *Hometown Santa Barbara*, the L.A. restaurant critic for *Westways*, and a sixth-generation Southern Californian who has written for everyone from the *Los Angeles Times* to *Bon Appetit*. A Pasadena resident, Colleen has been a Julienne customer for many years.

www.prospectparkbooks.com

Basil Friedman
FOOD STYLIST

With business and culinary degrees, Basil Friedman found work satisfaction elusive until he accidentally stumbled into a food photo shoot. A lightbulb went off in his head and Basil knew he had found his dream job. In the intervening years, he has styled cookbooks, magazine articles, advertisements, catalogs, Web-based food sites, and online cooking shows. The old adage of eating with your eyes is so true, says Basil. "If people look at a photograph of food I have styled and want to eat it, then my job is done."

www.basilstylist.com

Robin Turk
PROP STYLIST

Robin Turk, art director and stylist, collaborates with photographers and publishers on editorial and advertising assignments nationwide. Recent works involve art direction on the food network production of Giada De Laurentiis' shows *Giada @ Home* and *Everyday Italian*. Cookbooks include *The Bon Appetit Cookbook* and *Williams-Sonoma Outdoor Entertaining*. Robin says, "To know Sue is to instantly love Sue. To be part of her vision creating beautiful table settings filled with glorious foods is a moment I will treasure."

www.robinturk.com

Index

ACCOMPANIMENTS. See Side Dishes
Almonds
    Bisteeya with Chicken and Toasted
        Almonds, 143–44
    Chocolate Cranberry Torte with Frosted
        Cranberries and Gold Leaf, 167–68
    Cranberry Ice, 163
    Sugar-Crusted Nectarine, Blueberry
        and Toasted Almond Croustades, 89
Apples
    Apple Pie Cake with Whiskey Caramel
        Sauce, 85
    Braised Red Cabbage with Apples,
        Golden Raisins and Caraway Seeds, 153
    Cabbage, Apple and Thyme Soup, 55
    Celery Root, Apple and Radish Salad
        with Mustard Seed Vinaigrette, 67
    Crème Brûlée French Toast with
        Sautéed Apples, 19
    Wild Rice, Dried Apricots and Toasted
        Pecan Salad with Port Vinaigrette, 59
Apricots
    Chicken Strips with Ginger-Apricot
        Sauce, 72–73
    Croque Monsieur with Tomato-
        Apricot Chutney, 31–32
    Ginger-Apricot Sauce, 73
    Lamb Tagine with Orange, Dried
        Apricots and Prunes, 141
    Mustard Roasted Pork Tenderloin with
        Dried Apricots, Orange and Ginger
        Sauce, 151–52
    Sugar-Crusted Nectarine, Blueberry
        and Toasted Almond Croustades, 89
    Tomato-Apricot Chutney, 31–32
    Wild Rice, Dried Apricots and Toasted
        Pecan Salad with Port Vinaigrette, 59
Artichokes, 115
    Roasted Fennel with Baby Carrots,
        Haricot Verts, and Baby Artichokes, 121
Asparagus, 99
    Chopped Salad with Roast Chicken
        and Vegetables and Basil-Parsley

    Pesto, 37
    Grilled Shrimp, Asparagus, and Butter
        Lettuce Salad, 39
    Leek and Asparagus Strudel, 117
    Spinach Crusted Quiche with Roasted
        Vegetables, 26

BABY BACK PORK RIBS with Espresso
  Barbecue Glaze, 77
Bacon
    Candied Applewood Bacon, 23
    Open-Faced Omelet with Roasted
        Rosemary Potatoes, 21
    Roasted Corn and Cilantro Chowder, 56
Bananas, Hummingbird Cake with
  Pineapple, Pecans and, 83
Basil
    Basil-Parsley Pesto, 15, 32
    Chopped Salad with Roast Chicken and
        Vegetables and Basil-Parsley Pesto, 37
    Croque Monsieur with Tomato-
        Apricot Chutney, 31–32
    Tomato, Basil Pesto and Three-Cheese
        Strata, 75
Beans, 121
    Roasted Fennel with Baby Carrots,
        Haricot Verts and Baby Artichokes, 121
Beef, 69
    Beef Daube Provençal, 69
    Warm Filet of Beef Sandwich with
        Caramelized Onions, Gorgonzola
        Cream and Arugula on Seeded
        Sourdough, 33
Berries
    Blackberry Polenta Bread Pudding, 81
    Blueberry Pancakes with Lemon Curd, 22
    Chocolate Ganache Fondue with Long-
        Stem Strawberries, 107
    Coconut Macaroons with Chocolate
        Raspberry Ganache, 109
    Crème Brûlée French Toast, 19–20
    Fresh Berry Coulis, 20
    Lemon Soufflé Pudding Cake, 82

    Raspberry Cream Cheese Muffins, 27
    Raspberry Jam Hearts, 111
    Sugar-Crusted Nectarine, Blueberry
        and Toasted Almond Croustades, 89
Beverages
    Callebaut Hot Chocolate, 25
    Joseph's Limoncello, 131
Bisteeya with Chicken and Toasted
  Almonds, 143–44
Black Rice, 161
Blackberries
    Blackberry Polenta Bread Pudding, 81
    Lemon Soufflé Pudding Cake, 82
Blood Orange Sauce, 161–62
Blueberries
    Blueberry Pancakes with Lemon Curd, 22
    Lemon Soufflé Pudding Cake, 82
    Sugar-Crusted Nectarine, Blueberry
        and Toasted Almond Croustades, 89
Bourride with Grilled Vegetables and
  Saffron Aïoli, 35–36
Bread Puddings
    Blackberry Polenta Bread Pudding, 81
    Chicken and Mushroom Bread
        Pudding with Tarragon and Gruyère
        Cheese, 76
    Crème Brûlée French Toast with
        Crème Anglaise and Fresh Berry
        Coulis, 19–20
    Tomato, Basil Pesto and Three-Cheese
        Strata, 75
Breakfast Dishes
    Blueberry Pancakes with Lemon Curd, 22
    Callebaut Hot Chocolate, 25
    Candied Applewood Bacon, 23
    Crème Brûlée French Toast with
        Crème Anglaise and Fresh Berry
        Coulis, 19–20
    Espresso Coffee Cake, 29
    Maple Bran Muffins, 17
    Open-faced Omelet with Roasted
        Rosemary Potatoes and Chicken
        Sausage, 21

Raspberry Cream Cheese Muffins, 27
Spinach Crusted Quiche with Roasted
    Vegetables, 26
Brownies. See also Cookies
    Chocolate Crème de Menthe Bars, 105
    Chocolate Espresso Cream Cheese
        Bars, 94–95
    Chocolate Truffle Brownies, 106

CABBAGE
    Braised Red Cabbage with Apples,
        Golden Raisins and Caraway Seeds, 153
    Cabbage, Apple and Thyme Soup, 55
    Red Cabbage Slaw with Toasted
        Walnuts and Gorgonzola, 68
Cakes
    Apple Pie Cake with Whiskey Caramel
        Sauce, 85
    Espresso Coffee Cake, 29
    Hummingbird Cake with Banana,
        Pineapple and Pecans, 83
    Lemon Soufflé Pudding Cake, 82
    Spiced Pumpkin Cheesecake with
        Gingersnap Crust, 86–87
    Steamed Persimmon Pudding with
        Sherry Sabayon, 156–57
Callebaut Hot Chocolate, 25
Candied Applewood Bacon, 23
Capers
    Lentil Salad with Currants and
        Turmeric Vinaigrette, 65
    Mint-Caper Sauce, 119–20
    Parmesan-Crusted Swordfish
        with Lemon and Crispy Caper
        Sauce, 40–41
    Roasted Leg of Lamb with Gremolata
        Crust with Mint-Caper Sauce, 119–20
Caramel
    Honey-Caramel Sauce, 133
    Whiskey Caramel Sauce, 87
Carrots, 51
    Bourride with Grilled Vegetables and
        Saffron Aïoli, 35–36

Carrot Ginger Soup, 51
Roasted Cumin Carrots with Feta, 139
Roasted Fennel with Baby Carrots,
    Baby Artichokes and Haricot Verts, 121
Celery Root
    Celery Root, Apple and Radish Salad
        with Mustard Seed Vinaigrette, 67
    Celery Root Puree, 165
    Phyllo Cups with Celery Root Puree, 165
Chase, Sarah Leah, 91
Cheese
    Cabbage, Apple and Thyme Soup, 55
    Chicken and Mushroom Bread
        Pudding with Tarragon and Gruyère
        Cheese, 76
    Chocolate Espresso Cream Cheese
        Bars, 94–95
    Croque Monsieur with Tomato-
        Apricot Chutney, 31–32
    Gorgonzola Cream, 33
    Harvest Salad with Pears, Dried Figs,
        Baby Spinach and Cider Vinaigrette, 149
    Hummingbird Cake with Banana,
        Pineapple and Pecans, 83
    Orzo Salad with Feta, Mint and Green
        Onions, 61
    Parmesan-Crusted Swordfish with
        Lemon and Crispy Caper Sauce, 40–41
    Potato, Gruyère and Fennel Gratin, 155
    Raspberry Cream Cheese Muffins, 27
    Red Cabbage Slaw with Toasted
        Walnuts and Gorgonzola, 68
    Roasted Cumin Carrots with Feta, 139
    Roasted Potato Salad with Snow Peas,
        Parmesan, Lemon and Garlic, 63
    Spiced Pumpkin Cheesecake with
        Gingersnap Crust, 86–87
    Tomato, Basil Pesto, and Three-Cheese
        Strata, 75
    Tomato, Basil Pesto and Three-Cheese
        Strata, 75
    Warm Filet of Beef Sandwich with
        Caramelized Onions, Gorgonzola

Cream, and Arugula on Seeded
    Sourdough, 33
Cheesecake, Pumpkin, with Gingersnap
    Crust, 86–87
Cherries
    Cherry-Rhubarb Chutney, 79
    Chicken Breasts with Cherry-Rhubarb
        Chutney, 79
    Muscovy Duck Breasts with Spiced
        Pomegranate Sauce and Dried
        Cherries, 164
Chicken
    Bisteeya with Chicken and Toasted
        Almonds, 143–44
    Chicken and Mushroom Bread
        Pudding with Tarragon and Gruyère
        Cheese, 76
    Chicken Breasts with Cherry-Rhubarb
        Chutney, 79
    Chicken Strips with Ginger-Apricot
        Sauce, 72–73
    Chopped Salad with Roast Chicken
        and Vegetables and Basil-Parsley
        Pesto, 37
    Lemon-Herb Roasted Chicken in a
        Bread Basket, 57
    Linguine Chinois, 62
    Open-faced Omelet with Roasted
        Rosemary Potatoes and Chicken
        Sausage, 21
Chiles, 56
    Nectarine–Serrano Chile Salsa, 129
    Orange-Chipotle Vinaigrette, 71
    Roasted Corn and Cilantro
        Chowder, 56
    Salmon with Nectarine–Serrano Chile
        Salsa, 129
    Salmon with Pistachio and Dried
        Cranberry Crust and Orange-
        Chipotle Vinaigrette, 71
Chocolate, 25, 103
    Callebaut Hot Chocolate, 25
    Chocolate Cranberry Torte with Frosted

Cranberries and Gold Leaf, 167–68
Chocolate Crème de Menthe Bars, 105
Chocolate Espresso Cookies, 112
Chocolate Espresso Cream Cheese
  Bars, 94–95
Chocolate Festival, 103–13
Chocolate Ganache Fondue with Long-
  Stem Strawberries, 107
Chocolate Glaze, 94–95, 167–68
Chocolate Truffle Brownies, 106
Coconut Macaroons with Chocolate
  Raspberry Ganache, 109
Peppermint Shortbread Cookies, 113
Chopped Salad with Roast Chicken and
  Vegetables and Basil-Parsley Pesto, 37
Christmas Dishes, 159–68
Chocolate Cranberry Torte with Frosted
  Cranberries and Gold Leaf, 167–68
Cranberry Ice, 163
Muscovy Duck Breasts with Spiced
  Pomegranate Sauce and Dried
  Cherries, 164
Phyllo Cups with Celery Root Puree, 165
Chutneys
Cherry-Rhubarb Chutney, 79
Tomato-Apricot Chutney, 31
Cider Vinaigrette, 149
Cinnamon
Bisteeya with Chicken and Toasted
  Almonds, 143–44
Couscous with Cinnamon, Currants
  and Pine Nuts, 137
Orange Slices with Cinnamon and
  Orange Flower Water Syrup, 145
Citrus Fruits. See Lemons; Oranges
Coconut
Coconut Macaroons with Chocolate
  Raspberry Ganache, 109
Hummingbird Cake with Banana,
  Pineapple and Pecans, 83
Lemon Coconut Bars, 90
Coffee
Chocolate Espresso Cookies, 112

Chocolate Espresso Cream Cheese
  Bars, 94–95
Espresso Barbecue Sauce, 77
Espresso Coffee Cake, 29
Cole Slaw, 68
Red Cabbage Slaw with Toasted
  Walnuts and Gorgonzola, 68
Cookies. See also Brownies
Chocolate Espresso Cookies, 112
Coconut Macaroons with Chocolate
  Raspberry Ganache, 109
Crystallized Ginger Cookies, 93
Graham Cracker Chewy Bars, 91
Lemon Coconut Bars, 90
Peppermint Shortbread Cookies, 113
Raspberry Jam Hearts, 111
Corn
Chopped Salad with Roast Chicken
  and Vegetables and Basil-Parsley
  Pesto, 37
Roasted Corn and Cilantro Chowder, 56
Courgettes, Roasted, with Olive Oil, 130
Couscous with Cinnamon, Currants and
  Pine Nuts, 137
Cranberries
Chocolate Cranberry Torte with Frosted
  Cranberries and Gold Leaf, 167–68
Cranberry Ice, 163
Frosted Cranberries, 168
Mustard Roasted Pork Tenderloin with
  Dried Apricots, Orange and Ginger
  Sauce, 151–52
Salmon with Pistachio and Dried
  Cranberry Crust and Orange-
  Chipotle Vinaigrette, 71
Crème Anglaise, 20
Crème Brûlée French Toast with Crème
  Anglaise and Fresh Berry Coulis, 19–20
Croque Monsieur with Tomato-Apricot
  Chutney, 15, 31–32
Crystallized Ginger Cookies, 93
Currants
Couscous with Cinnamon, Currants

and Pine Nuts, 137
Lentil Salad with Currants and
  Turmeric Vinaigrette, 65
Wheat Berry Salad with Orange Zest,
  Pecans and Currants, 127
Wild Rice, Dried Apricots and
  Toasted Pecan Salad with Port
  Vinaigrette, 59

DESSERT SAUCES
Chocolate Glaze, 94–95, 167–68
Chocolate Raspberry Ganache, 109
Crème Anglaise, 20
Espresso Glaze, 29
Fresh Berry Coulis, 20
Honey-Caramel Sauce, 133
Lemon Curd, 22
Orange Flower Water Syrup, 145
Sherry Sabayon, 156–57
Whiskey Caramel Sauce, 87
Desserts. See also Bread Puddings;
  Brownies; Cakes; Cookies; Dessert
  Sauces
Cranberry Ice, 163
Grandma Jolly's Rhubarb Meringue
  Tarts, 123
Sugar-Crusted Nectarine, Blueberry
  and Toasted Almond Croustades, 89
Whole Peach Dumplings with Honey-
  Caramel Sauce, 133
Dressings
Cider Vinaigrette, 149
Mustard Seed Vinaigrette, 67
Orange-Chipotle Vinaigrette, 71
Port Vinaigrette, 59
Saffron Aïoli, 36
Turmeric Vinaigrette, 65
Vanilla Bean Vinaigrette, 39
Duck Breasts with Spiced Pomegranate
  Sauce and Dried Cherries, 164

EASTER DISHES, 115–23
Hummingbird Cake with Banana,

Pineapple and Pecans, 83

Leek and Asparagus Strudel, 117

Orzo Salad with Feta, Mint and Green
Onions, 61

Roasted Leg of Lamb with
Gremolata Crust with Mint-Caper
Sauce, 119–20

Eggs

Open-faced Omelet with Roasted
Rosemary Potatoes and Chicken
Sausage, 21

Spinach Crusted Quiche with Roasted
Vegetables, 26

Entrées, 69–79

Baby Back Pork Ribs with Espresso
Barbecue Glaze, 77

Beef Daube Provençal, 69

Chicken and Mushroom Bread
Pudding with Tarragon and Gruyère
Cheese, 76

Chicken Breasts with Cherry-Rhubarb
Chutney, 79

Chicken Strips with Ginger-Apricot
Sauce, 72–73

Lamb Tagine with Orange, Dried
Apricots and Prunes, 141

Muscovy Duck Breasts with Spiced
Pomegranate Sauce and Dried
Cherries, 164

Mustard Roasted Pork Tenderloin with
Dried Apricots, Orange and Ginger
Sauce, 151–52

Parmesan-Crusted Swordfish with
Lemon and Crispy Caper Sauce, 40–41

Roasted Leg of Lamb with Gremolata
Crust with Mint-Caper Sauce, 119–20

Salmon with Nectarine–Serrano Chile
Salsa, 129

Salmon with Pistachio and Dried
Cranberry Crust and Orange-
Chipotle Vinaigrette, 71

Seared Scallops with Blood Orange
Sauce and Black Rice Galettes, 161–62

Tomato, Basil Pesto, and Three-Cheese
Strata, 75

Espresso

Chocolate Espresso Cookies, 112

Chocolate Espresso Cream Cheese
Bars, 94–95

Espresso Barbecue Sauce, 77

Espresso Coffee Cake, 29

FENNEL

Grilled Potatoes, Fennel and Baby
Zucchini, 36

Potato, Gruyère and Fennel Gratin, 155

Roasted Fennel with Baby Carrots, Baby
Artichokes and Haricot Verts, 121

Figs

Harvest Salad with Pears, Dried Figs, Baby
Spinach and Cider Vinaigrette, 149

Orange Flower Water Syrup and, 145

Wild Rice, Dried Apricots and Toasted
Pecan Salad with Port Vinaigrette, 59

First Courses

Cabbage, Apple and Thyme Soup, 55

Fresh Pea Soup with Mint, 53

Seared Scallops with Blood Orange
Sauce and Black Rice Galettes, 161–62

Fish

Bourride with Grilled Vegetables and
Saffron Aïoli, 35–36

Parmesan-Crusted Swordfish with
Lemon and Crispy Caper Sauce, 40–41

Salmon with Nectarine–Serrano Chile
Salsa, 129

Salmon with Pistachio and Dried
Cranberry Crust and Orange-
Chipotle Vinaigrette, 71

Tomato-Apricot Chutney with, 31

Fondue, Chocolate Ganache, with Long-
Stem Strawberries, 107

French Dishes

Beef Daube Provençal, 69

Bourride with Grilled Vegetables and
Saffron Aïoli, 35–36

Crème Anglaise, 20

Croque Monsieur with Tomato-
Apricot Chutney, 31–32

Sherry Sabayon, 157

Sugar-Crusted Nectarine, Blueberry
and Toasted Almond Croustades, 89

French Toast, Crème Brûlée, with Crème
Anglaise and Fresh Berry Coulis, 19–20

GARTEN, INA, 25

Ginger

Carrot Ginger Soup, 51

Chicken Strips with Ginger-Apricot
Sauce, 72–73

Crystallized Ginger Cookies, 93

Ginger-Apricot Sauce, 73

Mustard Roasted Pork Tenderloin with
Dried Apricots, Orange and Ginger
Sauce, 151–52

Spiced Pumpkin Cheesecake with
Gingersnap Crust, 86–87

Gorgonzola Cream, 33

Graham Cracker Chewy Bars, 91

Grains

Black Rice, 161

Wheat Berry Salad with Orange Zest,
Pecans and Currants, 127

Wild Rice, Dried Apricots and Toasted
Pecan Salad with Port Vinaigrette, 59

Grandma Jolly's Rhubarb Meringue
Tarts, 123

Gremolata, Roasted Leg of Lamb with,
119–20

Grilled Dishes

Grilled Potatoes, Fennel and Baby
Zucchini, 36

Grilled Shrimp, Asparagus and Butter
Lettuce Salad with Mango-Papaya
Salsa and Vanilla Bean Vinaigrette, 39

HAM

Croque Monsieur with Tomato-
Apricot Chutney, 31–32

Open-Faced Omelet with Roasted
 Rosemary Potatoes, 21
Haricot Verts, Roasted Fennel with Baby
 Carrots, Baby Artichokes and, 121
Harvest Feast, 147–57
Harvest Salad with Pears, Dried Figs, Baby
 Spinach and Cider Vinaigrette, 149
Herbs. See Basil; Mint; Parsley; Rosemary
Holiday Dishes, 147–68
Hollywood Bowl picnic foods, 57, 125–33
Honey-Caramel Sauce, 133
Hummingbird Cake with Banana,
 Pineapple and Pecans, 83

JOHNSON, LADY BIRD, 4
Julienne, 7, 15, 49, 67, 99

LAMB, 61
 Lamb Tagine with Orange, Dried
  Apricots and Prunes, 141
 Roasted Leg of Lamb with Gremolata
  Crust with Mint-Caper Sauce, 119–20
Leek and Asparagus Strudel, 117
Lemons
 Blueberry Pancakes with Lemon Curd, 22
 Joseph's Limoncello, 131
 Lemon Coconut Bars, 90
 Lemon Curd, 22
 Lemon Soufflé Pudding Cake, 82
 Lemon-Herb Roasted Chicken in a
  Bread Basket, 57
 Parmesan-Crusted Swordfish with
  Lemon and Crispy Caper Sauce, 40–41
 Roasted Leg of Lamb with Gremolata
  Crust with Mint-Caper Sauce, 119–20
 Roasted Potato Salad with Snow Peas,
  Parmesan, Lemon and Garlic, 63
Lentil Salad with Currants and Turmeric
 Vinaigrette, 65
Lettuce
 Chopped Salad with Roast Chicken
  and Vegetables and Basil-Parsley
  Pesto, 37

Grilled Shrimp, Asparagus, and Butter
 Lettuce Salad with Mango-Papaya
 Salsa and Vanilla Bean Vinaigrette, 39
Limoncello, Joseph's, 131
Linguine Chinois, 62
Lunch Dishes, 31–41
 Bourride with Grilled Vegetables and
  Saffron Aïoli, 35–36
 Chopped Salad with Roast Chicken and
  Vegetables and Basil-Parsley Pesto, 37
 Croque Monsieur with Tomato-
  Apricot Chutney, 31–32
 Grilled Shrimp, Asparagus and Butter
  Lettuce Salad with Mango-Papaya
  Salsa and Vanilla Bean Vinaigrette, 39
 Parmesan-Crusted Swordfish with
  Lemon and Crispy Caper Sauce, 40–41
 Warm Filet of Beef Sandwich with
  Caramelized Onions, Gorgonzola
  Cream, and Arugula on Seeded
  Sourdough, 33

MAIN COURSES. SEE ENTRÉES
Mango-Papaya Salsa, 39
Maple Bran Muffins, 17
McGee, Harold, 32
Mint, 99
 Chocolate Crème de Menthe Bars, 105
 Fresh Pea Soup with Mint, 53
 Mint-Caper Sauce, 119–20
 Orzo Salad with Feta, Mint and Green
  Onions, 61
 Peppermint Shortbread Cookies, 113
 Roasted Leg of Lamb with Gremolata
  Crust with Mint-Caper Sauce, 119–20
Moroccan Dishes, 135–45
 Bisteeya with Chicken and Toasted
  Almonds, 143–44
 Couscous with Cinnamon, Currants
  and Pine Nuts, 137
 Lamb Tagine with Orange, Dried
  Apricots and Prunes, 141
 Orange Slices with Cinnamon and

Orange Flower Water Syrup, 145
 Roasted Cumin Carrots with Feta, 139
Muffins
 Maple Bran Muffins, 17
 Raspberry Cream Cheese Muffins, 27
Muscovy Duck Breasts with Spiced
 Pomegranate Sauce and Dried Cherries, 164
Mushroom and Chicken Bread Pudding
 with Tarragon and Gruyère Cheese, 76
Mustard
 Mustard Roasted Pork Tenderloin with
  Dried Apricots, Orange and Ginger
  Sauce, 151–52
 Mustard Seed Vinaigrette, 67

NECTARINES, 129
 Nectarine–Serrano Chile Salsa, 129
 Salmon with Nectarine–Serrano Chile
  Salsa, 129
 Sugar-Crusted Nectarine, Blueberry
  and Toasted Almond Croustades, 89
North African Dishes, 135–45
 Bisteeya with Chicken and Toasted
  Almonds, 143–44
 Couscous with Cinnamon, Currants
  and Pine Nuts, 137
 Lamb Tagine with Orange, Dried
  Apricots and Prunes, 141
 Orange Slices with Cinnamon and
  Orange Flower Water Syrup, 145
 Roasted Cumin Carrots with Feta, 139
Nuts. See specific nuts

OMELET, Open-faced, with Roasted
 Rosemary Potatoes and Chicken
 Sausage, 21
Onions
 Caramelized Onions, 33
 Orzo Salad with Feta, Mint and Green
  Onions, 61
 Warm Filet of Beef Sandwich with
  Caramelized Onions, Gorgonzola
  Cream and Arugula on Seeded

Sourdough, 33

Oranges
   Carrot Ginger Soup, 51
   Lamb Tagine with Orange, Dried
     Apricots and Prunes, 141
   Mustard Roasted Pork Tenderloin with
     Dried Apricots, Orange and Ginger
     Sauce, 151–52
   Orange Slices with Cinnamon and
     Orange Flower Water Syrup, 145
   Orange-Chipotle Vinaigrette, 71
   Seared Scallops with Blood Orange
     Sauce and Black Rice Galettes, 161–62
   Wheat Berry Salad with Orange Zest,
     Pecans and Currants, 127

Orzo Salad with Feta, Mint and Green
  Onions, 61

PANCAKES, Blueberry, with Lemon
  Curd, 22

Papaya-Mango Salsa, 39

Parmesan-Crusted Swordfish with Lemon
  and Crispy Caper Sauce, 40–41

Parsley, 32
   Basil-Parsley Pesto, 32
   Chopped Salad with Roast Chicken
     and Vegetables and Basil-Parsley
     Pesto, 37
   Roasted Leg of Lamb with Gremolata
     Crust with Mint-Caper Sauce, 119–20

Pasta
   Couscous with Cinnamon, Currants
     and Pine Nuts, 137
   Linguine Chinois, 62
   Orzo Salad with Feta, Mint and Green
     Onions, 61

Pastries. See also Brownies; Cakes;
  Cookies
   Sugar-Crusted Nectarine, Blueberry
     and Toasted Almond Croustades, 89
   Whole Peach Dumplings with Honey-
     Caramel Sauce, 133

Peaches, 125

Orange Flower Water Syrup and, 145
   Whole Peach Dumplings with Honey-
     Caramel Sauce, 133

Pears, 52, 89
   Harvest Salad with Pears, Dried Figs, Baby
     Spinach and Cider Vinaigrette, 149
   Roasted Red Pepper and Pear Soup, 52

Peas
   Fresh Pea Soup with Mint, 53
   Roasted Potato Salad with Snow Peas,
     Parmesan, Lemon and Garlic, 63

Pecans
   Carrot Ginger Soup, 51
   Graham Cracker Chewy Bars, 91
   Harvest Salad with Pears, Dried
     Figs, Baby Spinach and Cider
     Vinaigrette, 149
   Hummingbird Cake with Banana,
     Pineapple and Pecans, 83
   Wheat Berry Salad with Orange Zest,
     Pecans and Currants, 127
   Wild Rice, Dried Apricots and Toasted
     Pecan Salad with Port Vinaigrette, 59

Peppermint Shortbread Cookies, 113

Peppers. See also Chiles
   Orzo Salad with Feta, Mint and Green
     Onions, 61
   Roasted Red Pepper and Pear Soup, 52
   Spinach Crusted Quiche with Roasted
     Vegetables, 26

Persimmons, 156
   Steamed Persimmon Pudding with
     Sherry Sabayon, 156–57

Pestos
   Basil-Parsley Pesto, 32
   Chopped Salad with Roast Chicken
     and Vegetables and Basil-Parsley
     Pesto, 37
   Tomato, Basil Pesto and Three-Cheese
     Strata, 75

Phyllo Pastry
   Bisteeya with Chicken and Toasted
     Almonds, 143–44

Leek and Asparagus Strudel, 117
   Phyllo Cups with Celery Root Puree, 165

Picnic Foods, 125–33
   Chicken Strips with Ginger-Apricot
     Sauce, 72–73
   Crystallized Ginger Cookies, 93
   Joseph's Limoncello, 131
   Lemon-Herb Roasted Chicken in a
     Bread Basket, 57
   Red Cabbage Slaw with Toasted
     Walnuts and Gorgonzola, 68
   Roasted Baby Courgettes with Olive
     Oil, 130
   Salmon with Nectarine–Serrano Chile
     Salsa, 129
   Salmon with Pistachio and Dried
     Cranberry Crust and Orange-
     Chipotle Vinaigrette, 71
   Wheat Berry Salad with Orange Zest,
     Pecans and Currants, 127

Pine Nuts
   Basil-Parsley Pesto, 32
   Couscous with Cinnamon, Currants
     and Pine Nuts, 137
   Orzo Salad with Feta, Mint and Green
     Onions, 61

Pineapple
   Hummingbird Cake with Banana,
     Pineapple and Pecans, 83
   Mango-Papaya Salsa, 39

Pistachios, Salmon with Dried Cranberry
  Crust and, 71

Polenta Bread, 81

Pomegranates, 147
   Muscovy Duck Breasts with Spiced
     Pomegranate Sauce and Dried
     Cherries, 164

Pork
   Baby Back Pork Ribs with Espresso
     Barbecue Glaze, 77
   Candied Applewood Bacon, 23
   Mustard Roasted Pork Tenderloin with
     Dried Apricots, Orange and Ginger

Sauce, 151–52
Tomato-Apricot Chutney with, 31
Port Vinaigrette, 59
Potatoes
Grilled Potatoes, Fennel and Baby
Zucchini, 36
Open-faced Omelet with Roasted
Rosemary Potatoes and Chicken
Sausage, 21
Potato, Gruyère and Fennel Gratin, 155
Roasted Corn and Cilantro Chowder, 56
Roasted Potato Salad with Snow Peas,
Parmesan, Lemon and Garlic, 63
Roasted Rosemary Potatoes, 21
Prunes, Lamb Tagine with Orange, Dried
Apricots and, 141
Pumpkin Cheesecake with Gingersnap
Crust, 86–87

QUICHE, Spinach Crusted, with Roasted
Vegetables, 26

RADISH, Celery Root and Apple Salad, 67
Raisins
Braised Red Cabbage with Apples,
Golden Raisins and Caraway
Seeds, 153
Lamb Tagine with Orange, Dried
Apricots and Prunes, 141
Steamed Persimmon Pudding with
Sherry Sabayon, 156–57
Raspberries
Blackberry Polenta Bread Pudding, 20
Coconut Macaroons with Chocolate
Raspberry Ganache, 109
Crème Brûlée French Toast, 19–20
Fresh Berry Coulis, 20
Lemon Soufflé Pudding Cake, 82
Raspberry Cream Cheese Muffins, 27
Raspberry Jam Hearts, 111
Red Cabbage
Braised Red Cabbage with Apples,
Golden Raisins and Caraway Seeds, 153

Red Cabbage Slaw with Toasted
Walnuts and Gorgonzola, 68
Red Pepper and Pear Soup, 52
Rhubarb
Cherry-Rhubarb Chutney, 79
Grandma Jolly's Rhubarb Meringue
Tarts, 123
Rice
Black, 161
Seared Scallops with Blood Orange
Sauce and Black Rice Galettes, 161–62
Wild Rice, Dried Apricots and
Toasted Pecan Salad with Port
Vinaigrette, 59
Roasted Chicken in a Bread Basket, 57
Roasted Leg of Lamb with Gremolata
Crust with Mint-Caper Sauce, 119–20
Roasted Vegetables
Roasted Baby Courgettes with Olive
Oil, 130
Roasted Corn and Cilantro Chowder, 56
Roasted Cumin Carrots with Feta, 139
Roasted Fennel with Baby Carrots, Baby
Artichokes and Haricot Verts, 121
Roasted Potato Salad with Snow Peas,
Parmesan, Lemon and Garlic, 63
Roasted Red Pepper and Pear Soup, 52
Rosemary Potatoes, 21
Spinach Crusted Quiche, 26
Roberts, Michael, 15
Rosemary
Lemon-Herb Roasted Chicken in a
Bread Basket, 57
Roasted Rosemary Potatoes, 21

SAFFRON AÏOLI, 36
Salads, 59–68. See also Dressings
Celery Root, Apple and Radish Salad
with Mustard Seed Vinaigrette, 67
Chopped Salad with Roast Chicken
and Vegetables and Basil-Parsley
Pesto, 37
Grilled Shrimp, Asparagus and Butter

Lettuce Salad with Mango-Papaya
Salsa and Vanilla Bean Vinaigrette, 39
Harvest Salad with Pears, Dried Figs, Baby
Spinach and Cider Vinaigrette, 149
Lentil Salad with Currants and
Turmeric Vinaigrette, 65
Linguine Chinois, 62
Orzo Salad with Feta, Mint and Green
Onions, 61
Red Cabbage Slaw with Toasted
Walnuts and Gorgonzola, 68
Roasted Potato Salad with Snow Peas,
Parmesan, Lemon and Garlic, 63
Wheat Berry Salad with Orange Zest,
Pecans and Currants, 127
Wild Rice, Dried Apricots and
Toasted Pecan Salad with Port
Vinaigrette, 59
Salmon
Salmon with Nectarine–Serrano Chile
Salsa, 129
Salmon with Pistachio and Dried
Cranberry Crust and Orange-
Chipotle Vinaigrette, 71
Salsas
Mango-Papaya Salsa, 39
Nectarine–Serrano Chile Salsa, 129
Sandwiches
Croque Monsieur with Tomato-
Apricot Chutney, 31–32
Warm Filet of Beef Sandwich with
Caramelized Onions, Gorgonzola
Cream and Arugula on Seeded
Sourdough, 33
Sauces. See also Dessert Sauces
Basil-Parsley Pesto, 32
Blood Orange Sauce, 161–62
Cherry-Rhubarb Chutney, 79
Crispy Caper Sauce, 40–41
Espresso Barbecue Sauce, 77
Ginger-Apricot Sauce, 73
Mint-Caper Sauce, 119–20
Nectarine–Serrano Chile Salsa, 129

Saffron Aïoli, 36
Spiced Pomegranate Sauce, 164
Tomato-Apricot Chutney, 31–32
Scallops, Seared, with Blood Orange Sauce and Black Rice Galettes, 161–62
Sherry Sabayon, 156–57
Shortbread Cookies, Peppermint, 113
Shrimp
Bourride with Grilled Vegetables and Saffron Aïoli, 35–36
Grilled Shrimp, Asparagus and Butter Lettuce Salad with Mango-Papaya Salsa and Vanilla Bean Vinaigrette, 39
Side Dishes
Braised Red Cabbage with Apples, Golden Raisins and Caraway Seeds, 153
Couscous with Cinnamon, Currants and Pine Nuts, 137
Phyllo Cups with Celery Root Puree, 165
Potato, Gruyère and Fennel Gratin, 155
Roasted Rosemary Potatoes, 21
Snow Peas, Roasted Potato Salad with Parmesan, Lemon, Garlic and, 63
Soups
Bourride with Grilled Vegetables and Saffron Aïoli, 35–36
Cabbage, Apple and Thyme Soup, 55
Carrot Ginger Soup, 51
Fresh Pea Soup with Mint, 53
Roasted Corn and Cilantro Chowder, 56
Roasted Red Pepper and Pear Soup, 52
Spinach
Harvest Salad with Pears, Dried Figs, Baby Spinach and Cider Vinaigrette, 149
Spinach Crusted Quiche with Roasted Vegetables, 26
Splichal, Joachim, 2
Squash
Roasted Baby Courgettes with Olive Oil, 130
Spinach Crusted Quiche with Roasted Vegetables, 26

Steamed Persimmon Pudding with Sherry Sabayon, 156–57
Strawberries
Chocolate Ganache Fondue with Long-Stem Strawberries, 107
Fresh Berry Coulis, 20
Sugar-Crusted Nectarine, Blueberry and Toasted Almond Croustades, 89
Swordfish, Parmesan-Crusted, with Lemon and Crispy Caper Sauce, 40–41

TARTS, Grandma Jolly's Rhubarb Meringue, 123
Thanksgiving Dishes, 15, 147–57, 159
Braised Red Cabbage with Apples, Golden Raisins and Caraway Seeds, 153
Cranberry Ice, 163
Harvest Salad with Pears, Dried Figs, Baby Spinach and Cider Vinaigrette, 149
Mustard Roasted Pork Tenderloin with Dried Apricots, Orange and Ginger Sauce, 151–52
Potato, Gruyère and Fennel Gratin, 155
Steamed Persimmon Pudding with Sherry Sabayon, 156–57
Tomatoes
Tomato, Basil Pesto and Three-Cheese Strata, 75
Tomato-Apricot Chutney, 31–32
Turmeric Vinaigrette, 65

VANILLA BEAN VINAIGRETTE, 39
Vegetables. See also specific vegetables
Grilled Potatoes, Fennel and Baby Zucchini, 36
Roasted Fennel with Baby Carrots, Baby Artichokes and Haricot Verts, 121
Spinach Crusted Quiche with Roasted Vegetables, 26
Vinaigrettes
Cider Vinaigrette, 149
Mustard Seed Vinaigrette, 67
Orange-Chipotle Vinaigrette, 71

Port Vinaigrette, 59
Turmeric Vinaigrette, 65
Vanilla Bean Vinaigrette, 39

WALNUTS
Apple Pie Cake with Whiskey Caramel Sauce, 85
Chocolate Espresso Cookies, 112
Chocolate Espresso Cream Cheese Bars, 94–95
Chocolate Truffle Brownies, 106
Raspberry Jam Hearts, 111
Red Cabbage Slaw with Toasted Walnuts and Gorgonzola, 68
Spiced Pumpkin Cheesecake with Gingersnap Crust, 86–87
Steamed Persimmon Pudding with Sherry Sabayon, 156–57
Wheat Berry Salad with Orange Zest, Pecans and Currants, 127
Whiskey Caramel Sauce, 87
Wild Rice, Dried Apricots and Toasted Pecan Salad with Port Vinaigrette, 59
Winter Celebration, 159–69

ZUCCHINI
Chopped Salad with Roast Chicken and Vegetables and Basil-Parsley Pesto, 37
Grilled Potatoes, Fennel and Baby Zucchini, 36
Roasted Baby Courgettes with Olive Oil, 130
Spinach Crusted Quiche with Roasted Vegetables, 26